WHAT HAPPENS NEXT

A TRAVELER'S GUIDE THROUGH
THE END OF THIS AGE

A SIX-SESSION BIBLE STUDY ON THE END TIMES

MAX LUCADO

WITH SAM O'NEAL

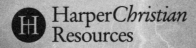

HarperChristian
Resources

What Happens Next Bible Study Guide
© 2024 by Max Lucado

Requests for information should be addressed to:
HarperChristian Resources, 3900 Sparks Dr. SE, Grand Rapids, Michigan 49546

ISBN 978-0-310-17275-8 (softcover)
ISBN 978-0-310-17282-6 (ebook)

First Printing July 2024 / Printed in the United States of America

CONTENTS

A NOTE FROM MAX

This is a study on the end times. Now, when I say this, I know it will cause different reactions among different people. Some will likely dive into this study with excitement, hoping to learn more about future events. But others will approach this study with reluctance, wondering why they need to dedicate the next six weeks of their lives to poking into what the Bible says about the future. After all, aren't there more pressing issues to deal with in the present?

Not surprisingly, I'm a member of the first camp. I'm genuinely interested in what happens next. Maybe because I'm getting older. My hourglass has more sand on the bottom than on the top. Consequently, eschatology (the study of end times) has become a fascination for me. I really want to know what's around the corner.

I also find that understanding the future empowers me to face the present. Paul had this same opinion. He wrote, "Forgetting what is behind and straining toward what is ahead, I press on toward the goal to win the prize" (Philippians 3:13–14). The best of life is yet to be. Got challenges in the here-and-now? Then ponder what is to come.

This is why I'm delighted that the Bible offers so much relevant information on the topic. So much to discover and to ponder. Yet I offer this word of advice to myself and others who are fascinated about the end times: *Don't ignore the Giver by focusing on the gift.* Or, to put it another way: *Don't ignore the Planner by focusing on the plan.* Yes, the Bible has much to say about the future of our world, the end of history, and the glorious span of eternity that lies beyond. But God didn't give us those glimpses just so that we could better understand the future. He helps us see the plan to invite us to spend eternity with him.

Now, to those in the second camp—those who are more hesitant to study the end times for any reason—let me offer this advice: *Setting your eyes on the future is good for you.* In fact, it's necessary. Don't just take my word for it. Listen again to Paul:

"Since, then, you have been raised with Christ, set your hearts on things above, where Christ is, seated at the right hand of God. Set your minds on things above, not on earthly things" (Colossians 3:1-2).

Set your minds on things above. Your soul needs hourly gazes into the life to come. You need to know what your departed loved ones are doing. You need to envision the rapture and the millennium. You need to picture your eternal home and the face of God. Why? Because heaven is the green vegetable in the spiritual diet. It makes us whole. It keeps us healthy.

So read on. Study on. Ponder on. And be consumed with the things above.

— MAX LUCADO

HOW TO USE THIS GUIDE

The world today feels fragile. So much uncertainty and unrest. Wars. Natural disasters. Polarization. Addiction. Anxiety. Loneliness. Epidemics. Pandemics. All these troubles that you are experiencing in the present can cause you to look toward the future with concern. *Why is this happening right now? What does it all mean?*

What will happen next?

The world often seems as if it is spiraling out of control. But rest assured that *nothing* is happening on this planet that is a surprise to God. "He knows everything" (1 John 3:20). What's more, he hasn't left you in the dark about his plans. He has given you a map to follow. A divine itinerary in the pages of his Word. The more familiar you become with that itinerary, the more you will be able to face the problems of this life by focusing on the promises of the next.

This is the purpose of this study—to help you understand what God said would happen next as the end times approach and how to view those events through the eyes of faith rather than fear. Before you begin, know that there are a few ways you can go through this material. You can experience this study with others in a group (such as a Bible study, Sunday school class, or other gathering), or you can go through the content on your own. Either way, the videos are available to view at any time by following the instructions provided with this study guide.

GROUP STUDY

Each of the sessions in this study is divided into two parts: (1) a group study section, and (2) a personal study section. The group study section provides a basic framework on how to open your time together, get the most out of the video content, and discuss the key ideas that were presented in the teaching. Each session includes the following:

- **Welcome:** A short opening note about the topic of the session for you to read on your own before you meet as a group.
- **Connect:** A few icebreaker questions to get you and your group members thinking about the topic and interacting with each other.
- **Watch:** An outline of the key points covered in each video teaching along with space for you to take notes as you watch each session.
- **Discuss:** Questions to help you and your group reflect on the teaching material presented and apply it to your lives.
- **Respond:** A short personal exercise to help reinforce the key ideas.
- **Pray:** A place for you to record prayer requests and praises for the week.

If you are doing this study in a group, make sure you have your own copy of the study guide so you can write down your thoughts, responses, and reflections in the space provided—and so you have access to the videos via streaming. You will also want to have a copy of the *What Happens Next* book, as reading it alongside this guide will provide you with deeper insights. (See the notes at the beginning of each group session and personal study section on which chapters of the book you should read before the next group session.)

Finally, keep these points in mind:

- **Facilitation:** If you are doing this study in a group, you will want to appoint someone to serve as a facilitator. This person will be responsible for starting the video and keeping track of time during discussions and activities. If *you* have been chosen for this role, there are some resources in the back of this guide that can help you lead your group through the study.

- **Faithfulness:** Your group is a place where tremendous growth can happen as you reflect on the Bible, ask questions, and learn what God is doing in other people's lives. For this reason, be fully committed and attend each session so you can build trust and rapport with the other members.

- **Friendship:** The goal of any small group is to serve as a place where people can share, learn about God, and build friendships. So seek to make your group a "safe place." Be honest about your thoughts and feelings, but also listen carefully to everyone else's thoughts, feelings, and opinions. Keep anything personal that your group members share in confidence so that you can create a community where people can heal, be challenged, and grow spiritually.

If you are going through this study on your own, read the opening Welcome section and reflect on the questions in the Connect section. Watch the video and use the outline provided to help you take notes. Finally, personalize the questions and exercises in the Discuss and Respond sections. Close by recording any requests you want to pray about during the week.

PERSONAL STUDY

The personal study is for you to work through on your own during the week. Each exercise is designed to help you explore the key ideas you uncovered during your group time and delve into passages of Scripture that will help you apply those principles to your life. Go at your own pace, doing a little each day—or tackle the material all at once. Remember to spend a few moments in silence to listen to whatever God might be saying to you.

Note that if you are doing this study as part of a group, and you are unable to finish (or even start) these personal studies for the week, you should still attend the group time. Be assured that you are still wanted and welcome even if you don't have your "homework" done. The group studies and personal studies are intended to help you hear what God wants you to hear and apply what he is saying to your life. So . . . as you go through this study, be listening for him to speak to you about what will happen next for you and for those you love.

HEAVEN'S
TIME LINE

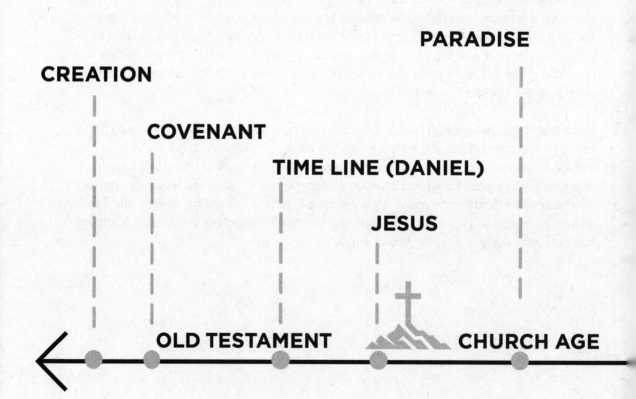

CREATION

PARADISE

COVENANT

TIME LINE (DANIEL)

JESUS

OLD TESTAMENT

CHURCH AGE

NOT TO SCALE

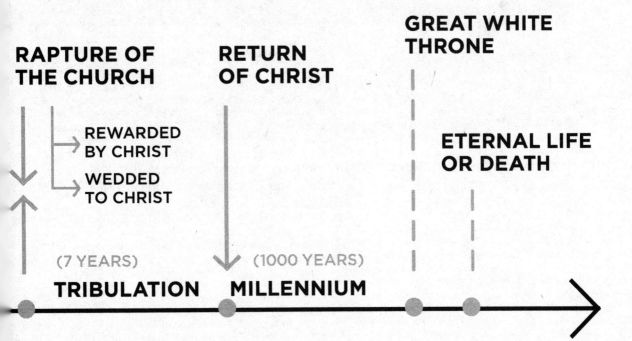

RAPTURE OF THE CHURCH

→ REWARDED BY CHRIST

→ WEDDED TO CHRIST

(7 YEARS)
TRIBULATION

RETURN OF CHRIST

(1000 YEARS)
MILLENNIUM

GREAT WHITE THRONE

ETERNAL LIFE OR DEATH

WEEK 1

BEFORE GROUP MEETING	Read chapters 1–3 in *What Happens Next* Read the Welcome section (page 3)
GROUP MEETING	Discuss the Connect questions Watch the video teaching for session 1 Discuss the questions that follow as a group Do the closing exercise and pray (pages 3–8)
STUDY 1	Complete the personal study (pages 10–12)
STUDY 2	Complete the personal study (pages 13–15)
STUDY 3	Complete the personal study (pages 16–18)
CATCH UP AND READ AHEAD (BEFORE WEEK 2 GROUP MEETING)	Read chapters 4–5 in *What Happens Next* Complete any unfinished personal studies (page 19)

MADE TO REIGN

Repent, then, and turn to God, so that your sins may be wiped out, that times of refreshing may come from the Lord, and that he may send the Messiah, who has been appointed for you—even Jesus. Heaven must receive him until the time comes for God to restore everything, as he promised long ago through his holy prophets.

ACTS 3:19-21

HEAVEN'S
TIME LINE

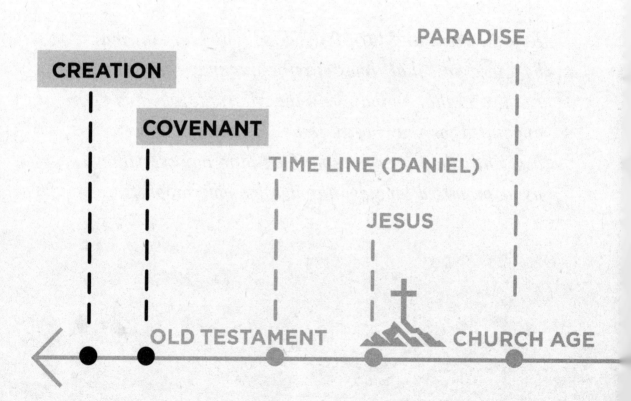

PARADISE

CREATION

COVENANT

TIME LINE (DANIEL)

JESUS

OLD TESTAMENT

CHURCH AGE

NOT TO SCALE

WELCOME | READ ON YOUR OWN

Theologians call it a "super sign." It took place on May 14, 1948. On that day in history, Jewish leaders gathered in the city of Tel Aviv to declare that Israel would now be a sovereign nation. Obviously, the moment was a big deal for the Jewish people. For the first time in two thousand years, they had their own Jewish state. Yet the moment was also a big deal for those who follow biblical prophecy, for the reestablishment of Israel as a nation is a major prophetic theme in God's Word.

The restoration of Israel opened the door for key events of the end times to occur: the rapture, rise of the Antichrist, tribulation, millennium, final judgment, our eternal home in heaven. We are going to explore each of those events in this study. However, we are going to start not by looking at the events of the end but by going back to the beginning. *Eschatology*, the study of end things, begins with *protology*, the study of first things.

Why is this important? The reason is because we need to have a foundation of what God has done in the past if we want to understand what he is going to do in the future. We need to have a correct understanding of his character, as revealed by his words and actions in the past, before we look at the end-times events that will occur in the future. When we do this, four convictions about God arise in the pages of his Word.

The first is that God created human beings to reign with him. His original intent for humanity was to rule as his regents over creation. The second is that God made covenants (or promises) with his people. The covenants reveal his intentions for us in the past, the present, and the future. We will explore these two themes in this session.

CONNECT | 15 MINUTES

If you or any of your group members don't know each other, take a few minutes to introduce yourselves. Then discuss one or both of the following questions:

- Why did you decide to join this study? What do you hope to learn?

  — *or* —

- On a scale of 1 (low) to 10 (high), how would you rate your interest in biblical prophecy and the end times? Explain your response.

WATCH | 20 MINUTES

Watch the video for this session, which you can access by playing the DVD or through streaming (see the instructions that have been provided with this study guide). Below is an outline of the key points covered during the teaching. Record any key concepts that stand out to you.

OUTLINE

I. We can think of our journey toward eternity in terms of moving from *known* to *known*.
   - A. The Bible tells us that we started our trip in the garden of Eden.
   - B. The Bible tells us that we will end our trip with Jesus in the New Jerusalem.
   - C. But there are a lot of questions and confusion about what will happen in between.
   - D. Fortunately, God has given us an itinerary of *what happens next* in his Word.

II. Our story begins with God instructing Adam and Eve to have dominion over creation.
   - A. Unfortunately, the first humans sinned and gave up their authority to Satan.
   - B. So God suspended his garden-of-Eden plan—but he did not abandon it.
   - C. God's storyline concludes with us ruling with him in a perfect world.

III. We will not only experience a renewal of Eden in eternity but also a renewal of authority.
   - A. God has not only promised that we will reign but has also provided us with a number of covenants in his Word.
   - B. God's first covenant, as we have already seen, was with Adam and Eve.
   - C. God's Edenic covenant is still leading us to a future time when we will rule and reign over a perfected earth.

IV. God's covenant with Abraham consisted of a *seed* and *soil* promise.
   - A. The *seed* promise refers to God making Abraham's descendants into a great nation.
   - B. The *soil* promise refers to specific borders the Jews will occupy in the land of Israel.
   - C. God has fulfilled the seed promise, so we can expect him to fulfill the soil promise.

V. God also made a covenant with David and to his people through Jeremiah.
   - A. God promised David that one of his descendants would rule over his kingdom forever.
   - B. God revealed through the prophet Jeremiah that there would be a spiritual revival of the Jewish people.
   - C. God's plan for the future includes the fulfillment of each of these promises.

NOTES

DISCUSS | 35 MINUTES

Discuss what you just watched by answering the following questions.

1. When it comes to considering what the Bible says about what will happen as we approach the end times, it often seems that different denominations, churches, ministry leaders, and believers all have a different vision of "what happens next." What have you been taught about the next steps in God's plan for the future?

2. In this week's teaching, four covenants were mentioned that have governed God's plan for the past, present, and future—covenants with Adam and Eve, with Abraham, with David, and through the prophet Jeremiah. Which of those covenants feels most relevant to your life? Why?

3. Ask someone to read aloud Hebrews 2:6–8. The covenant that God established with Adam and Eve included a promise of *dominion*—a call for them to reign and rule over creation. What does the author of Hebrews say about the current status of this promise? Where do you see humanity attempting to exercise dominion over the world today?

4. Invite someone to read aloud Genesis 12:1–3 and Genesis 15:18–21. God promised that he would make Abraham's *seed* (or descendants) into a great nation, which he has fulfilled. God also promised that Abraham's descendants would occupy a certain amount of *soil* or land (all of modern-day Israel as well as parts of Egypt, Syria, Lebanon, and Iraq), which has not yet been fulfilled. What does this reveal about God's plans for Israel in the future?

5. Ask someone to read Luke 1:32–33. God's covenant with David included a promise that someone from his "house" would sit on his throne and rule over his kingdom forever. What did Gabriel say to Mary to indicate this would be Jesus? How has this session added to your understanding of Jesus' role as the Messiah?

RESPOND | 10 MINUTES

It is important to emphasize that God's plans for the future are not new. Rather, they are based on the foundation of the days that have already passed. In particular, what we will experience at the end of history is strongly connected to what Adam and Eve first experienced at the beginning of history. Take a few minutes on your own to review God's original design for humanity as expressed in the following passage and then answer the questions that follow.

> ²⁶ Then God said, "Let us make mankind in our image, in our likeness, so that they may rule over the fish in the sea and the birds in the sky, over the livestock and all the wild animals, and over all the creatures that move along the ground."
>
> ²⁷ So God created mankind in his own image,
>   in the image of God he created them;
>   male and female he created them.
>
> ²⁸ God blessed them and said to them, "Be fruitful and increase in number; fill the earth and subdue it. Rule over the fish in the sea and the birds in the sky and over every living creature that moves on the ground."
>
> GENESIS 1:26-28

Circle any words that speak directly to God's original plan for humanity. How would you summarize that original plan? In other words, based on what you read in this passage, what role did God intend for human beings to carry out within his creation?

In your own words, what does it mean to be created "in the image of God" (verse 27)? How should that reality impact both your present and your future?

PRAY | 10 MINUTES

When it is time to close this session, take a moment to acknowledge God's control over history—including the past, present, and future. Specifically acknowledge his control over what will happen next in your life and in the lives of your group members. Ask for God's wisdom and clarity to help you navigate the remaining sessions of this study. Finally, use the space below to write down any requests so that you and your group members can continue to pray about them in the week ahead.

NAME   **REQUEST**

PERSONAL STUDY

You are on a journey with your fellow group members toward a better understanding of "what happens next" as it relates to the end times. As a reminder, the only reason you can know anything at all about this subject is because God has revealed a great deal about his plans in his Word. For that reason, the personal study portion of each session will help you take a deeper look at certain passages and principles that are the most critical to an understanding of the end times. As you work through each of these exercises, be sure to write down your responses to the questions. (If you are engaging this study as part of a group, you will be given a few minutes to share your insights at the start of the next session.) If you are reading *What Happens Next* alongside this study, first review the introduction and chapters 1–3 of the book.

HOPE FOR THE FUTURE

Did you know that the Bible makes almost seven hundred references to heaven?[1] It's true. Where you spend eternity is a critical priority to God. And when you study what those Scriptures say, you come across two major themes that keep resurfacing.

The first is that the future God has in store for his people should fill them with hope. Thank God this is true! But have you noticed how little hope is present in the present—even among Christians? People today seem miserable, confused, lonely, and without peace. A necessary ingredient for emotional and spiritual well-being seems to be missing in our world today: *hope*.

God reminds you again and again in his Word to fix your mind on the hope of the future as a tonic to overcome the hopelessness of today. We see this in Jesus' interactions with his disciples on the night of his arrest shortly before he went to the cross. During the Last Supper, Jesus said to his disciples, "Do not let your hearts be troubled. You believe in God; believe also in me. My Father's house has many rooms; if that were not so, would I have told you that I am going there to prepare a place for you? And if I go and prepare a place for you, I will come back and take you to be with me that you also may be where I am" (John 14:1–3). In what could have been a moment of fear and dread, Jesus lifted the disciples' thoughts not to the persecution in their immediate future but to the reality of their eternal home.

A second theme is that the future is all about *Jesus*. The most consequential moment in human history occurred when Jesus stepped into our world as a living, breathing human being—and then died on the cross for our sins. Likewise, the most consequential moment in our future will be the day when Jesus returns to this world. We call this the second coming of Christ, and the Bible speaks of it as a guarantee (see 1 Thessalonians 4:16–17).

Consider what the angels told the disciples after Jesus ascended into heaven: "Men of Galilee . . . why do you stand here looking into the sky? This same Jesus, who has been taken from you into heaven, will come back in the same way you have seen him go into heaven" (Acts 1:11). You can count on Christ's return, which is why the future is all about him.

1. To what degree do you currently feel hopeful about the future?

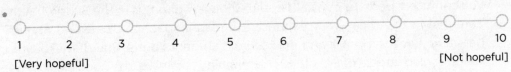

| 1 | 2 | 3 | 4 | 5 | 6 | 7 | 8 | 9 | 10 |

[Very hopeful]   [Not hopeful]

2. What are the biggest factors currently contributing to your level of hope? (In other words, what are the biggest factors responsible for the score you gave?)

The Christian lives life on tiptoe, ever searching the skies. We awaken with the thought, *Perhaps today!* Our hope is centered on the bodily return of Christ. We are looking to a new age in which Jesus will be crowned as the rightful King and we will serve as his grateful servants. All of history is headed to the great day that will inaugurate an endless era of justice, joy, and glory.

In one of his earliest sermons, Peter declared: "The Lord will . . . send Jesus, the One he chose to be the Christ. But Jesus must stay in heaven until the time comes when all things will be made right again" (Acts 3:19–21 NCV).

Things will be made right again. Does that assurance not speak to the heavy heart? Weary of racism? *Things will be made right.* Weary of child abuse? *Things will be made right.* Weary of terrorists wreaking terror? Rulers pillaging the poor? Scandal infecting the church? *Things . . . will . . . be . . . made . . . right.*[2]

---

3. When have you recently felt weary about the state of our present world? How does the promise found in Acts 3:21 give you hope for the future?

Maybe you are a bit leery about this discussion. End-times studies have left you confused, perhaps cynical. I understand. Prophecy is to the Bible what the Serengeti is to Africa—vast, expansive, and intimidating. It's a world of numbers and symbols, bears and tigers. Most students prefer the domesticated, well-traveled streets of Scripture: the teachings of Jesus, the doctrines of Paul, the biographies of the Patriarchs. Prophecy intimidates many Bible students.

It infatuates others. If Bible prophecy is the Serengeti, some Christians are big-game hunters. They never leave the bush. They find prophecy on every page, symbolism in every story, and clues in every verse. They can be a great source of help, but they can also be stubbornly opinionated. Prophetic experts tend to be very confident; they walk with a game-hunter swagger. They always seem to know (and enjoy knowing) what others don't.

Somewhere in between these two positions is a healthy posture. Believers who avoid utter ignorance on one hand and total arrogance on the other. Who seek what God intends: a deep-seated confidence that our tomorrow is in our Lord's hands. The purpose of prophecy is to empower the saint with a sense of God's sovereignty.[3]

4. Read Romans 10:9 and Ephesians 2:8. Part of preparing for the future is making sure you are certain of your destination. Based on these verses, what is necessary to make certain you are "good to go" in terms of eternal life?

5. Where do you stand when it comes to considering the end times? What are your personal goals for participating in this study? In what specific areas would you like to grow—or what specific information do you hope to glean as you work through these pages?

EDEN FULFILLED

As you discussed during this week's group time, God created human beings to reign and rule over creation. He gave Adam and Eve dominion over the garden of Eden and told them to "be fruitful and increase in number; fill the earth and subdue it" (Genesis 1:28). God's intent was for their progeny to expand over the earth—and expand human dominion over all the earth.

Humanity was created to reign. Not by ourselves, of course. We were created to reign as regents of God. His plan was for those who had been created in his image to exercise his authority over his world. As God declared, "Let us make mankind in our image, in our likeness, so that they may rule over the fish in the sea and the birds in the sky, over the livestock and all the wild animals, and over all the creatures that move along the ground" (verse 26).

Sadly, that plan was disrupted and distorted by the fall. When Adam and Eve chose to believe the enemy's lies, they allowed the serpent to usurp their authority. They lost the ability to reign as perfect representatives of their perfect Creator. They became separated from him—literally cast out of the garden and banished from his presence (see 3:23)—and thus separated from their ability to "rule over" the world in a life-giving way. (More on that below.) Yet that doesn't mean God's original plan has been invalidated or abandoned. Far from it!

The painful truth for us as human beings is that our past and our present have been stained by sin. This cannot be denied. Just look at the daily news! Our world is a place of violence, fear, hopelessness, anxiety, greed, laziness, lust, and pride—to name just a few such vices. These things are not just "out there" in the general mill of humanity. We find them "in here"—we deal with them each and every day inside of our own hearts.

Yet the truth is that our past and our present have also been touched by God's redemptive plan. He has opened the door for forgiveness and salvation. In doing so, he has recreated a pathway for us to rule once more. There is a forecast of "reign" in our future!

1. Review Genesis 1:26–30. Summarize the idea of God giving human beings "dominion" over the created world. What should that look like on a practical level?

2. This concept of having dominion doesn't exist only on a grand scale. We were also created to have dominion and be stewards over our families and in our communities. When have you recently felt the desire to set things in order or make things right in your corner of the world? What happened as a result?

> [1] Now the serpent was more crafty than any of the wild animals the Lord God had made. He said to the woman, "Did God really say, 'You must not eat from any tree in the garden'?"
>
> [2] The woman said to the serpent, "We may eat fruit from the trees in the garden, [3] but God did say, 'You must not eat fruit from the tree that is in the middle of the garden, and you must not touch it, or you will die.'"
>
> [4] "You will not certainly die," the serpent said to the woman. [5] "For God knows that when you eat from it your eyes will be opened, and you will be like God, knowing good and evil."
>
> [6] When the woman saw that the fruit of the tree was good for food and pleasing to the eye, and also desirable for gaining wisdom, she took some and ate it. She also gave some to her husband, who was with her, and he ate it. [7] Then the eyes of both of them were opened, and they realized they were naked; so they sewed fig leaves together and made coverings for themselves.
>
> GENESIS 3:1–7

3. Circle any words or phrases in that passage that strike you as important or interesting. What were the temptations that led Adam and Eve to disobey God?

4. Sin has affected humanity in a broad way—in a *cosmic* way. But it also touches our lives as individuals each day. What causes you to feel especially frustrated or undermined by the reality of sin as you look at the state of the world today?

Instead of ruling the world, we feel ruled by the world. We see creation in a state of corruption, eruption, and pollution. Heat waves. Wildfires. Hurricanes. Earthquakes. Famines. "The whole creation has been groaning as in the pains of childbirth right up to the present time" (Romans 8:22). Something is awry. What's more, we don't see male and female behaving as partners, but often as rivals.

What happened? Sin happened. Rebellion happened. Satan happened. Greed happened. A villain infiltrated the garden. He convinced the couple that the garden, resplendent and abundant, was inadequate. Eden was not enough for the couple. They wanted to be like God. And God, who knows what is best for creation, said, "No." He temporarily suspended the garden-of-Eden plan. But he did not cancel it. He did not abandon it. He certainly did not abandon us.[4]

5. The person you were created to be still matches (or at least points to) God's original plan for you to rule and reign as his representative on this earth. What qualities, abilities, and talents do you possess that allow you to be a force for good in your corner of the world?

EDEN RECLAIMED

The pages of the Bible are filled with the story of salvation. You may have heard of the four "movements" defining that story: (1) creation, (2) fall, (3) redemption, and (4) restoration (or glorification). These are critical themes that drive history forward in ways that have concrete implications for your life as an individual.

You have already looked at the first and second movement. At *creation*, God set up human beings to rule and reign over creation. This was our high calling—but we blew it. The subsequent *fall* introduced sin into the world, which has thrown everything into chaos ever since—chaos for the plants, and the animals, and all the earth . . . and chaos for humanity. Chaos not just for our morality and our relationships but also for that high calling. We lost the chance to do what we were created to do. But thankfully, we did not lose it forever.

This is where the third movement, *redemption*, comes into the story. We talk often about God's redemption and incredible gift of grace toward us—and rightfully so! The life, death, and resurrection of Jesus Christ is the cornerstone not only of your faith but also of your future. In the words of the apostle Paul, "If Christ has not been raised, your faith is futile; you are still in your sins. Then those also who have fallen asleep in Christ are lost. If only for this life we have hope in Christ, we are of all people most to be pitied" (1 Corinthians 15:17-19).

But let's not forget about the fourth movement. Let's not forget about *restoration*. God's plan for our eternal future involves much more than sitting on a cloud strumming harps, as the cartoonists would want us to believe. No, God's plan involves a restoration (and even an expansion) of his original design for Eden. "You are worthy to take the scroll and to open its seals," sang the elders in John's vision of the end times, "because you were slain, and with your blood you purchased for God persons from every tribe and language and people and nation." That's us. That's the church. And notice what comes next: "You have made them to be a kingdom and priests to serve our God, and they will reign on the earth" (Revelation 5:9-10).

What awaits us in the next phase of human history is a version of Eden reclaimed in which we once again rule and reign as regents of Christ.

1. Imagine you are back in the garden of Eden. Specifically, try to place yourself in a world that is untainted by the corruption of sin. What are some ways the world would be different than everything you've experienced in life up to this point?

[18] Consequently, just as one trespass resulted in condemnation for all people, so also one righteous act resulted in justification and life for all people. [19] For just as through the disobedience of the one man the many were made sinners, so also through the obedience of the one man the many will be made righteous. [20] The law was brought in so that the trespass might increase. But where sin increased, grace increased all the more, [21] so that, just as sin reigned in death, so also grace might reign through righteousness to bring eternal life through Jesus Christ our Lord.

ROMANS 5:18-21

2. The apostle Paul refers to the actions of both Adam and Jesus in this passage. Where do you see similarities between Adam and Jesus? What are the major differences between them?

3. The story of the Bible includes not just God's offer of redemption (movement 3) but also his relentless pursuit of his people. God refused to give up on his creation, including human beings, and promised to restore them (movement 4). What are some ways that you have experienced God's pursuit of you? How has he called you and called out to you?

God's dream has never changed. Consider his invitation: "Look! I have been standing at the door, and I am constantly knocking. If anyone hears me calling him and opens the door, I will come in and fellowship with him and he with me. I will let everyone who conquers sit beside me on my throne, just as I took my place with my Father on his throne when I had conquered" (Revelation 3:20–21 TLB). God's storyline concludes with you, me, all his children living, ruling, dining, and serving with him in a perfect world.[5]

4. Read Revelation 3:20–21. What is God's invitation to you today? What emotions do you experience when you think about the future reality of reigning with Christ?

5. In the same way that God formed Adam, so he has formed you. He has hand-crafted you to have an important role in his kingdom. What obstacles are currently hindering or preventing you from accepting the reality that you are unique, special, and wonderful?

CATCH UP AND READ AHEAD

Connect with a fellow group member and discuss some of the key insights from this session. Use any of the following prompts to help guide your discussion.

- What did you like best from the content in this session, including both the group study and personal study? Why?
- Where do you see a loss of hope causing problems in today's culture? How have you experienced hopelessness in your own life?
- One of the central claims of this session is that human beings were created *to* reign with God and we *will* reign with God in the future. God's original plan will be reclaimed. How do you respond to that premise?
- What do you remember about the four covenants that have guided God's plans for the past, present, and future? (These would be covenants with Adam and Eve, with Abraham, with David, and through Jeremiah.)
- What do you feel most excited to explore in the sessions ahead? Why?

Use this time to go back and complete any of the study and reflection questions from previous days that you weren't able to finish. Make a note below of any revelations you've had and reflect on any growth or personal insights you've gained.

Read chapters 4–5 in *What Happens Next* before the next group gathering. Use the space below to make note of anything that stands out to you or encourages you.

WEEK 2

BEFORE GROUP MEETING	Read chapters 4–5 in *What Happens Next* Read the Welcome section (page 23)
GROUP MEETING	Discuss the Connect questions Watch the video teaching for session 2 Discuss the questions that follow as a group Do the closing exercise and pray (pages 23-28)
STUDY 1	Complete the personal study (pages 30–32)
STUDY 2	Complete the personal study (pages 33–36)
STUDY 3	Complete the personal study (pages 37–40)
CATCH UP AND READ AHEAD (BEFORE WEEK 3 GROUP MEETING)	Read chapters 6–8 in *What Happens Next* Complete any unfinished personal studies (page 41)

GOD'S PLAN FOR THE AGES

While I was still in prayer, Gabriel . . . came to me in swift flight about the time of the evening sacrifice. He instructed me and said to me, "Daniel, I have now come to give you insight and understanding. As soon as you began to pray, a word went out, which I have come to tell you, for you are highly esteemed. Therefore, consider the word and understand the vision."

DANIEL 9:21–23

HEAVEN'S
TIME LINE

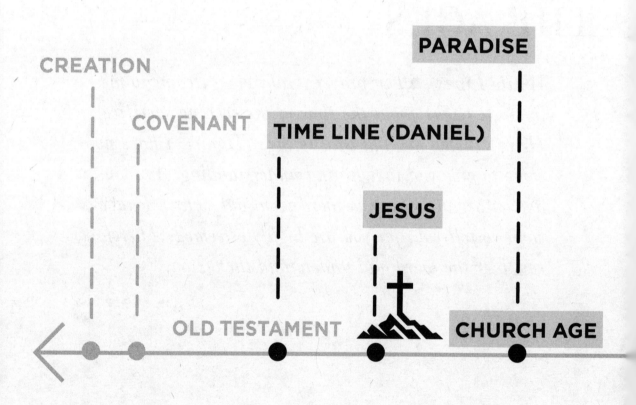

CREATION

COVENANT

PARADISE

TIME LINE (DANIEL)

JESUS

OLD TESTAMENT

CHURCH AGE

NOT TO SCALE

WELCOME | READ ON YOUR OWN

Here's a question worth considering: *What is the purpose of the Bible?* Scripture represents God's Word—that is what it *is*. But what is it *for*? Many would answer that question by saying God gave us the Bible to teach us, which is true. Scripture is, first and foremost, God's revelation of himself. It helps us understand who God is and what he values. It also helps us understand who we are and what we should value.

Scripture also teaches about the reality of sin and our need for salvation. It reveals the means of that salvation is through the death and resurrection of Christ. Others will add that God gave us the Bible as a record of history. Scripture reveals the reality of creation and the tragedy of the fall. It tells us the stories of Adam, Abraham, Moses, David, the prophets, and many more. It also describes the launch and the early history of the church, which gives us a historical foundation as modern believers.

There are many other reasons why God has blessed us with the Bible. But in this session, we are going to focus on one that has a direct connection with the theme of this study. Namely, that God gave us the Bible not only to describe history that occurred in the past but also to reveal his plans for the entirety of history.

The Bible not only reveals what *did* happen but also gives us a picture of what *will* happen. In this session, we will look at a passage of Scripture that many have labeled as "the backbone of biblical prophecy." We will also explore the importance of the millennium when it comes to building an understanding of God's plan for history.

CONNECT | 15 MINUTES

If you or any of your group members don't know each other, take a few minutes to introduce yourselves. Then discuss one or both of the following questions:

- What is something that spoke to you in last week's personal study that you would like to share with the group?

  — *or* —

- How do you typically respond to the prophecies contained in the Bible? To what degree do those prophecies interest you?

WATCH | 20 MINUTES

Now watch the video for this session. Below is an outline of the key points covered during the teaching. Record any key concepts that stand out to you.

OUTLINE

I. Although the book of Revelation is the best-known source of information on the end times, the prophecy in Daniel 9 is actually the ideal starting point for the topic.
   A. Daniel was a Hebrew youth when he was taken as a captive to Babylon.
   B. It was there in exile that Daniel received a vision from the angel Gabriel.
   C. Scholars have called this passage the "backbone" of biblical prophecy.

II. Gabriel spoke three prophecies to Daniel in the midst of his vision.
   A. The first promised a spiritual revival for the Jews that would occur in 490 years.
   B. The second foretold the coming of the Messiah, which would take place 483 years after the declaration to rebuild Jerusalem.
   C. The third is connected to those final seven "years," which represent the tribulation.

III. The split in Daniel's vision between 483 years and 490 years is important.
   A. The 483 years ended with Jesus' triumphal entry into Jerusalem.
   B. However, when the Jewish people rejected Jesus as their promised Messiah, God "pressed pause" on the countdown of history.
   C. This countdown will resume—and these final seven years will be the tribulation.

IV. There are three primary ways of interpreting what the Bible says about the millennium.
   A. The *amillennial* position says that the Bible's references to a thousand-year period are figurative and that we are currently experiencing the millennium.
   B. The *postmillennial* position also views the thousand years as symbolic—this position states that Jesus' return will occur after the millennium.
   C. The *premillennial* position takes the thousand years as literal. The time line indicates a rapture, then the tribulation, then the second coming of Christ, then the millennium.

V. The premillennial position has several advantages when you look at what the Bible says.
   A. God will honor his covenants (Adam and Eve, Abraham, David, Jeremiah).
   B. A literal millennium also fulfills many biblical prophecies that refer to a future Christ-led kingdom that is established here on earth.

NOTES

DISCUSS | 35 MINUTES

Discuss what you just watched by answering the following questions.

1. Take a moment to review Daniel 9:20–27 as a group. This passage, considered by many scholars to be "the backbone of biblical prophecy," contains a vision that stretches out to many points in human history. What caught your attention in these verses? What questions came to mind when you read the passage?

2. In Gabriel's first prophecy to Daniel, he stated, "God has ordered four hundred ninety years for your people and your holy city for these reasons: to stop people from turning against God; to put an end to sin; to take away evil; to bring in goodness that continues forever; to bring about the vision and prophecy; and to appoint a most holy place" (verse 24 NCV). What specific events are mentioned or foreshadowed in this prophecy?

3. Gabriel's prophecy pointed forward to the exact day that Jesus rode into Jerusalem on a colt and presented himself as the Messiah (see Matthew 21:1–11). Yet so many people of the day missed it! As you consider this, what are some of the reasons we miss what God is trying to tell us today?

4. The millennium is important in God's plan for the future. How would you summarize what the millennium is and where it fits on the time line of history?

5. People in the church hold three main views about the millennium: *amillennialism*, *postmillennialism*, and *premillennialism*. What are the differences between these viewpoints? What are some of the reasons as to why the premillennial position makes sense in light of God's broader plans and promises?

RESPOND | 10 MINUTES

Jesus was certainly aware of Daniel's prophecy regarding the Messiah when he made the "Triumphal Entry" into Jerusalem. He understood that he was the fulfillment of Daniel's prophecy, and so he offered himself to the Jewish people. As you read the passage below about the events of that day, keep in mind that many people in the crowd understood what was happening. They recognized their Messiah had arrived and called out their praises to him.

> [37] When he came near the place where the road goes down the Mount of Olives, the whole crowd of disciples began joyfully to praise God in loud voices for all the miracles they had seen:
> [38] "Blessed is the king who comes in the name of the Lord!" "Peace in heaven and glory in the highest!"
> [39] Some of the Pharisees in the crowd said to Jesus, "Teacher, rebuke your disciples!"
> [40] "I tell you," he replied, "if they keep quiet, the stones will cry out."
>
> LUKE 19:37–40

God's plan doesn't only apply to "the ages" but also to your life as an individual. How would you describe God's plan for your life right now? What is he asking you to do or learn or be?

As you think about God's plans for you in the present, try to project them out into the future. Where do you see God leading or calling you in the next five years? Ten years? Twenty years?

PRAY | 10 MINUTES

Conclude this session by thanking God for his sovereignty and control over history. No matter what has happened throughout the centuries, God has promised, "Never will I leave you; never will I forsake you" (Hebrews 13:5). Praise God that you and your group members are protected and loved as part of his plan—and say yes to your place in his plan. Use the space below to write down any requests so that you and your group members can continue to pray about them in the week ahead.

NAME | REQUEST

PERSONAL STUDY

In the first session, we looked at two themes that serve as the foundation of this study: (1) human beings were intended to have dominion over creation, and (2) God's overarching plan for history is buttressed by covenants—including those made to Adam and Eve, Abraham, David, and God's people through Jeremiah. In this session, we are exploring the final foundational themes: (3) God has given us a time line for history in his Word, and (4) the pathway of history is leading to a future period known as the millennium, when we will experience a restored and expanded version of the garden of Eden. As you work through the exercises, write down your responses to the questions, as you will be given a few minutes to share your insights at the start of the next session if you are doing this study with others. If you are reading *What Happens Next* alongside this study, first review chapters 4–5 in the book.

A TIME LINE OF HISTORY

Daniel 9:20–27 offers a time line of history that is miraculous on several levels. This time line alone offers proof of the divine nature of Scripture, given that Gabriel's vision predicted the arrival of Jesus in Jerusalem to the *exact day*, even though that prophecy was recorded several hundred years before the time of Christ.

The time line tells us several other important truths about God's plan for history. First, the end of that time line will arrive with a spiritual revival among the Jewish people. As Gabriel said, "God has ordered four hundred ninety years for your people and your holy city for these reasons: to stop people from turning against God; to put an end to sin; to take away evil; to bring in goodness that continues forever; to bring about the vision and prophecy; and to appoint a most holy place" (verse 24 NCV). When Daniel's 490 years have come to completion, the Jewish people will return to God. They will embrace Jesus as their Messiah.

Second, Gabriel spoke of not only the appearance of the Messiah but also his subsequent death—and the later destruction of Jerusalem itself. "After the four hundred thirty-four years the appointed leader will be killed; he will have nothing. The people of the leader who is to come will destroy the city and the holy place" (verse 26 NCV). Jesus' death and resurrection took place around AD 33, while the destruction of Jerusalem occurred in AD 70.

Third, Gabriel's prophecy looked forward to the tribulation—a seven-year period when God will pour out his judgment against all who rebel against him. Gabriel declared of that time, "[The Antichrist] will make firm an agreement with many people for seven years. He will stop the offerings and sacrifices after three and one-half years. A destroyer will do blasphemous things until the ordered end comes to the destroyed city" (verse 27 NCV).

Thankfully, as we will see in a later session, the church will be raptured before the events of the tribulation. But importantly, there is a gap between Jesus' death—which occurred on the 483rd year of Gabriel's prophecy—and the final seven years, which are the tribulation. God pressed pause on his time line after the Jews rejected their Messiah. We are living in that pause right now, which is often called the "church age."

1. The prophecy that the angel Gabriel gave to Daniel included a spiritual revival among the Jewish people. How would you describe the current relationship between the church and the Jewish people? In what ways are those two groups connected and disconnected?

---

13 When Jesus came to the region of Caesarea Philippi, he asked his disciples, "Who do people say the Son of Man is?"

14 They replied, "Some say John the Baptist; others say Elijah; and still others, Jeremiah or one of the prophets."

15 "But what about you?" he asked. "Who do you say I am?"

16 Simon Peter answered, "You are the Messiah, the Son of the living God."

17 Jesus replied, "Blessed are you, Simon son of Jonah, for this was not revealed to you by flesh and blood, but by my Father in heaven."

MATTHEW 16:13–17

---

2. The prophecy that Gabriel delivered to Daniel also pointed forward to the arrival of the Messiah. How did Peter indicate in this passage that he understood Jesus to be the fulfillment of all the Old Testament prophecies concerning the Messiah? What are some of the ways Jesus' appearance has shaped our world in the centuries since his resurrection?

Hard times are coming. The Antichrist, the tribulation, the abomination that causes desolation—these are foreboding events. But if you are in Christ, you won't have to experience them. God will come for his church before the dark days begin. That event is commonly called the rapture. Jesus, with the power of a king and the kindness of a savior, will extract his children prior to the seven years of evil. The question is . . . will you be like those who missed the time stamp of Jesus in his day and refused to recognize him as Messiah? Or will you be ready for the rescue?[6]

3. Read Ezekiel 18:20–23. No matter how you try to parse the pages of Scripture, you cannot avoid the fact that the human race is heading toward judgment. A time is coming when evil will be fully punished. What does God say about "the one who sins" in this passage? But what is the outcome for those who choose to accept Jesus as their Messiah?

4. Based on what you learned during the group time and your own study of Scripture, create a time line of history in the space below. Start with creation and end with the millennium, and then add in ages and events (both past and future) that you feel are significant.

5. It can be tempting for Christians to want to insert present events into God's time line—for instance, pondering whether this person or that person in the news could potentially be the Antichrist. As students of Scripture, how can we handle our limited knowledge of the future in a way that is helpful and responsible?

THE IMPORTANCE OF PROPHECY

We have looked at what the biblical time line tells us from Daniel 9, including the cues and clues it provides for human history. Now let's explore *why* Gabriel's prophecies are important in the here and now. Why should these prophecies matter to you?

First, they reveal that you can trust biblical prophecy. Remember, the words recorded in Daniel's book were written several hundred years before the incarnation of Jesus, yet those words declared the exact day when Christ would present himself in Jerusalem. Those same words promised that Jesus would be killed and that even Jerusalem would be destroyed. All those prophecies came true as well. There are many other examples of biblical prophecy that have proven true—including the restoration of Israel as a nation in 1948, which we mentioned earlier in this study. All of this demonstrates that you can trust the Bible. Just as important, you can trust the One who gave you the Bible. God has proven himself trustworthy.

Second, understanding the truths of God's biblical time line will allow you to be prepared for what is coming next on that time line. Unfortunately, *what happens next* isn't pretty. Daniel 9 offers an introduction to the Antichrist and the tribulation, and those harbingers of chaos will not erupt in the middle of a peaceful world. Things are going to get *worse* before they get *better*. Yet because you know that, you can be prepared.

Third, Daniel's prophetic promises allow you to feel secure about your future—both your earthly future and your eternal one. Yes, there are tough times coming, but you know how it turns out. God wins, which means you win, which means you don't have to be burdened with anxiety about the future. You can embrace the security of trusting the future to the One who shaped it at the beginning of time.

In other words, you can confidently say with King David, "The LORD is my strength and my shield; my heart trusts in him, and he helps me. My heart leaps for joy, and with my song I praise him. The LORD is the strength of his people, a fortress of salvation for his anointed one. Save your people and bless your inheritance; be their shepherd and carry them forever" (Psalm 28:7–9).

1. Followers of Jesus have literally staked their eternal destiny on the truth of God's Word. Your hope for eternal life rests in your belief that God's Word is true. What helps you to trust in the Bible as the foundation for your eternal future?

[1] "At that time the kingdom of heaven will be like ten virgins who took their lamps and went out to meet the bridegroom. [2] Five of them were foolish and five were wise. [3] The foolish ones took their lamps but did not take any oil with them. [4] The wise ones, however, took oil in jars along with their lamps. [5] The bridegroom was a long time in coming, and they all became drowsy and fell asleep.

[6] "At midnight the cry rang out: 'Here's the bridegroom! Come out to meet him!'

[7] "Then all the virgins woke up and trimmed their lamps. [8] The foolish ones said to the wise, 'Give us some of your oil; our lamps are going out.'

[9] "'No,' they replied, 'there may not be enough for both us and you. Instead, go to those who sell oil and buy some for yourselves.'

[10] "But while they were on their way to buy the oil, the bridegroom arrived. The virgins who were ready went in with him to the wedding banquet. And the door was shut.

[11] "Later the others also came. 'Lord, Lord,' they said, 'open the door for us!'

[12] "But he replied, 'Truly I tell you, I don't know you.'

[13] "Therefore keep watch, because you do not know the day or the hour."

MATTHEW 25:1–13

2. In this parable, Jesus commended the five virgins who took oil with them and were prepared for the bridegroom's return. What was Jesus' point as it relates to his followers? Why is it important to understand and be ready for *what happens next* on God's time line?

3. The prophetic promises of God in Scripture can help you feel secure about your future—both your earthly and eternal one. However, salvation and eternal life are not the only promises found in the pages of God's Word! Look up the verses below and then record the specific promise that God has made to you.

Passage	Promise
Psalm 55:22	
Jeremiah 29:12	
Matthew 11:28	
Romans 8:26	
Hebrews 4:16	

4. Paul writes that Jesus, "having disarmed the powers and authorities . . . made a public spectacle of them, triumphing over them by the cross" (Colossians 2:15). Christ has already won the final confrontation with the forces of evil. God's judgment has already been rendered against evil. It waits only to be carried out, which means you're on the winning team. How can that truth help you in your battles against the enemy today?

[1] Everyone who believes that Jesus is the Christ is born of God, and everyone who loves the father loves his child as well. [2] This is how we know that we love the children of God: by loving God and carrying out his commands. [3] In fact, this is love for God: to keep his commands. And his commands are not burdensome, [4] for everyone born of God overcomes the world. This is the victory that has overcome the world, even our faith. [5] Who is it that overcomes the world? Only the one who believes that Jesus is the Son of God.

1 JOHN 5:1-5

5. John states that everyone born of God has overcome the world, which means that everyone who has placed their faith in Jesus Christ has victory over the forces of evil—both in themselves and in the world. How have you experienced this kind of victory in your life? Where would you like to experience this kind of victory in the weeks to come?

P.O.W.E.R.

There is a lot of debate within the church about precisely *what* the millennium is and *when* it will take place. This week, you examined three of the primary views: amillennial, postmillennial, and premillennial. The amillennial position holds that the millennium is figurative and we are currently experiencing it. The postmillennial position also views the thousand years as symbolic and states that Jesus' return will occur after the millennium. The premillennial position takes the thousand years of the millennium as literal. There are many compelling reason to favor this view, which can be summed up with the acronym P.O.W.E.R.

Promises of God: The premillennial view takes into account the promises in Scripture that are yet unfulfilled. For example, God promised that Abraham's descendants would inhabit a specific plot of land: "To your descendants I give this land, from the Wadi of Egypt to the great river, the Euphrates" (Genesis 15:18). This promise has not yet been fulfilled, but it will be fulfilled during the millennium.

Overthrow of Satan: Scripture promises Satan will be cast down and confined in the abyss for a thousand years. It's clear to see that hasn't happened yet. This is another prophecy that will take place during the golden age of the millennium.

Word-for-Word Interpretation: In Revelation 20:1-7, John uses the phrase "thousand years" six times to describe the future period when Satan is bound. Other prophecies, like Jeremiah's that the Babylonian exile would last for seventy years (see Jeremiah 25:11), are taken literally. So why not take John's number literally?

Early Church Fathers: The early church fathers largely understood the Scriptures to teach a literal understanding of the millennium—they saw it as a literal period of one thousand years. This includes some early teachers who trained under the apostles. So we should probably listen to them.

Resurrections: John specifically mentioned two resurrections that will take place in the age to come. The first applies to Christians who will be raised to life or taken up to heaven at the rapture. The second applies to unbelievers who will be raised at the final judgment. Those two resurrections match a premillennial framework very well.

1. Endorsing premillennialism, postmillennialism, or amillennialism doesn't make a difference when it comes to your salvation. Given this, what are some of the reasons as to why it can be helpful to grapple with those three approaches to Scripture? What is at stake if you don't grapple with the question of the millennium?

There are a collection of prophecies in Scripture that fit neither the present age nor our heavenly state. Here is an example: "No longer will babies die when only a few days old. No longer will adults die before they have lived a full life. No longer will people be considered old at one hundred! Only the cursed will die that young!" (Isaiah 65:20 NLT). Isaiah foresaw an era in which newborns won't die and life spans will stretch into centuries. This is far different from the present age, but it's also an inaccurate description of our eternal state when death shall be discontinued. Apparently heaven's itinerary includes a stage in history that is far greater than the status quo but far less than our final home. The millennium fits this description.[7]

2. Take a look at Isaiah 11:6–9. This prophecy portends a unique chapter in human history. It sounds like heaven. But when you read Isaiah 11:10–11, you find that those verses look forward to the same prophetic period, but it does not appear that the eternal state has yet begun. Do you think what Isaiah was describing in verses 6–9 is actually the millennium? How do you respond to these kinds of promises in the Bible of a golden age here on earth?

3. Read Daniel 9:1–3. Notice in this passage that Daniel's prayer was prompted by his reading of Jeremiah's prophecies. What did Daniel understand about how long the "desolation of Jerusalem" (the Jewish exile) would last? How does this argue for a more literal word-for-word interpretation of Scripture when it comes to understanding biblical prophecy?

⁶ Then they gathered around him and asked him, "Lord, are you at this time going to restore the kingdom to Israel?"

⁷ He said to them: "It is not for you to know the times or dates the Father has set by his own authority. ⁸ But you will receive power when the Holy Spirit comes on you; and you will be my witnesses in Jerusalem, and in all Judea and Samaria, and to the ends of the earth."

⁹ After he said this, he was taken up before their very eyes, and a cloud hid him from their sight.

ACTS 1:6-9

4. This was Jesus' final conversation with his disciples before he ascended into heaven. How does the disciples' question reflect their belief in a *literal* kingdom on earth ruled by the Messiah? How does Jesus' answer add to your understanding of such a kingdom?

5. Use the chart below to fill in the acronym for P.O.W.E.R. Which of these categories of evidence feels most important or significant to you when it comes to viewing the millennium as a literal thousand-year reign of Jesus on earth? Why?

P	
O	
W	
E	
R	

CATCH UP AND READ AHEAD

Connect with a fellow group member and discuss some of the key insights from this session. Use any of the following prompts to help guide your discussion.

- What ideas or concepts felt confusing to you in the content of this session? What questions would you like to have answered?
- How confident do you feel in your ability to process and understand the prophecies in Daniel 9:20–27? What is most striking to you in those verses?
- This session addressed several promises from God that will be fulfilled during the millennium. Which of those promises do you find most exciting?
- How would you describe our current place in God's prophetic calendar? What are we experiencing in history—and what is next?
- On a scale of 1 (low) to 10 (high), how important is it to study and form opinions on doctrines like the millennium? Explain your answer.

Use this time to go back and complete any of the study and reflection questions from previous days that you weren't able to finish. Make a note below of any revelations you've had and reflect on any growth or personal insights you've gained.

Read chapters 6–8 in *What Happens Next* before the next group gathering. Use the space below to make note of anything that stands out to you or encourages you.

WEEK 3

BEFORE GROUP MEETING	Read chapters 6–8 in *What Happens Next* Read the Welcome section (page 45)
GROUP MEETING	Discuss the Connect questions Watch the video teaching for session 3 Discuss the questions that follow as a group Do the closing exercise and pray (pages 45–50)
STUDY 1	Complete the personal study (pages 52–54)
STUDY 2	Complete the personal study (pages 55–57)
STUDY 3	Complete the personal study (pages 58–60)
CATCH UP AND READ AHEAD (BEFORE WEEK 4 GROUP MEETING)	Read chapters 9–11 in *What Happens Next* Complete any unfinished personal studies (page 61)

THE RESCUE AND THE REWARDS

For the Lord himself will come down from heaven, with a loud command, with the voice of the archangel and with the trumpet call of God, and the dead in Christ will rise first. After that, we who are still alive and are left will be caught up together with them in the clouds to meet the Lord in the air. And so we will be with the Lord forever.

1 THESSALONIANS 4:16-17

HEAVEN'S
TIME LINE

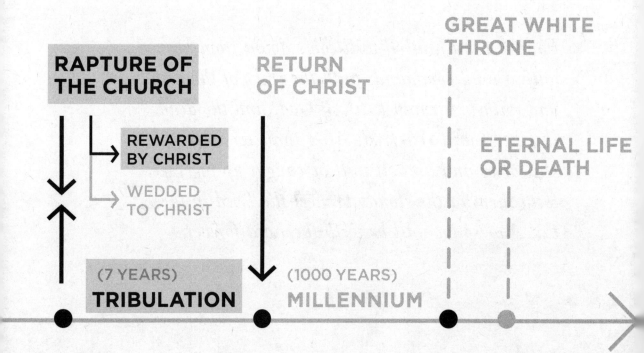

RAPTURE OF
THE CHURCH

RETURN
OF CHRIST

GREAT WHITE
THRONE

REWARDED
BY CHRIST

WEDDED
TO CHRIST

ETERNAL LIFE
OR DEATH

(7 YEARS)
TRIBULATION

(1000 YEARS)
MILLENNIUM

NOT TO SCALE

WELCOME | READ ON YOUR OWN

We all love a good rescue story. We love to read accounts of people in dire situations who are miraculously rescued. This is true not only in the world of books, movies, and television but also in the realm of everyday life.

Just consider some of the news reports of rescues that have gripped the public in recent times. In 1987, the world watched as rescuers worked for fifty-six hours to rescue a baby named Jessica who had fallen into a well. In 2010, the public followed the story of thirty-three trapped miners in Chile who, after two months, were successfully pulled to safety. In 2018, it was the rescue of a junior association soccer team from a cave in Thailand that captivated the world. The twelve members of the team and their coach had become trapped after a heavy rainfall flooded the cave.

Followers of Jesus are bound for a similar kind of rescue. As we move into the end times, the Bible reveals that things will go from bad to worse. The situation will become dire for God's people. As Jesus said of these times, "Nation will rise against nation, and kingdom against kingdom. There will be famines and earthquakes in various places. All these are the beginning of birth pains" (Matthew 24:7–8).

But then, right before the Antichrist sparks chaos on an even grander scale, Christ will come to save his people. Just like the rescuers in the news stories, Jesus will pull us out of the pit this world has become and take us to safety. Not only that, but his rescue will be followed by the delivery of incredible rewards. Ready to hear more?

CONNECT | 15 MINUTES

Get this session started by choosing one or both of the following questions to discuss together as a group:

- What is something that spoke to you in last week's personal study that you would like to share with the group?

— or —

- Think of the way we often describe Jesus as our "Savior." What does that title reveal about his nature and character?

WATCH | 20 MINUTES

Now watch the video for this session. Below is an outline of the key points covered during the teaching. Record any key concepts that stand out to you.

OUTLINE

I. It's time to answer the immediate question at the heart of this study: *What happens next?*

   A. In the time line of God's plan for history, the rapture is humanity's next stop.

   B. At some point in the future, upon the signal of Christ, the living followers of Jesus will be taken up and transported into the presence of their Savior.

   C. Believers who died before the rapture will be taken up as well.

II. God has history on hold until the full number of his flock passes through the gate.

   A. Jesus will come with "a loud command"—a command issued with authority.

   B. We will hear "the trumpet call"—Jesus' signal that it is time for us to march away.

   C. We will be *physically* present with Jesus and will be healed, renewed, and restored.

III. There are several different viewpoints in the church as to when the rapture will take place.

   A. Some believe that the rapture of the church will take place *before* the seven-year period of chaos known as the tribulation, some believe it will happen in the *middle* of the tribulation, and some believe it will happen *after* the tribulation.

   B. Jesus compared the moment of the rapture to the rescues of Noah and Lot.

   C. The rapture of the church is presented in the pages of Scripture as a reason for comfort and assurance, not fear and anxiety.

IV. After the rapture, believers will experience the judgment seat of Christ.

   A. The judgment seat of Christ is not about *salvation* but about *recognition*.

   B. Our deeds do not contribute to our salvation, but they do inform our recognition.

   C. Believers in Christ will be rewarded based on their works on earth.

V. The Bible mentions five crowns that we will offer back to Jesus in gratitude and praise.

   A. The crown of self-control (see 1 Corinthians 9:25).

   B. The crown of influence (see 1 Thessalonians 2:19).

   C. The crown of life (see James 1:12).

   D. The crown of righteousness (see 2 Timothy 4:7–8).

   E. The crown of glory (see 1 Peter 5:4 and 2 Corinthians 4:17).

NOTES

DISCUSS | 35 MINUTES

Discuss what you just watched by answering the following questions.

1. In recent years, the rapture has received notice in our culture as the subject of movies, TV shows, and book series. What comes to mind for you when you picture the rapture? How would you describe the idea of the rapture—and what will take place during it—to someone who has never heard of it before?

2. Read aloud 1 Thessalonians 4:13–18. What stands out to you in these verses? Note that if you are a believer in Christ, you will experience the rapture if it occurs during your lifetime. You will be physically taken up to be with Jesus in the clouds. What emotions do you experience when you think about that possibility?

3. Now read Matthew 24:37–39 and Luke 17:28–30. Jesus compared the moment of the rapture to the rescues of Noah and Lot. Noah felt no raindrops. Lot felt no brimstone. This would support the idea that the rapture will occur *before* the tribulation. What are some other examples that come to mind of how God has rescued his people throughout Scripture? How has he rescued you in your life?

4. Paul wrote, "We must all appear before the judgment seat of Christ, so that each of us may receive what is due us for the things done while in the body, whether good or bad" (2 Corinthians 5:10). The judgment seat of Christ will be a place of reward and acclamation, not one of condemnation. We will be rewarded based on our work for God's kingdom. What types of "good deeds" do you find easy to practice? Which ones are more difficult?

5. In Paul's day, athletes would stand before the *bēma,* an elevated seat on which the judge or emperor sat, and receive a crown (or laurel) of reward.[8] The Bible mentions five crowns: (1) self-control, (2) influence, (3) life, (4) righteousness, and (5) glory. What are some of the examples used in the teaching for how you obtain these crowns? How do you respond to the reality that Jesus will one day give you a crown for your good works on earth?

RESPOND | 10 MINUTES

The Olivet Discourse is a powerful sermon that Jesus delivered just a few days before his betrayal, death, and resurrection. In this message, Jesus talked about what life will be like in the days leading up to the rapture. Underline the phrase "birth pains" in this passage below. In the same way labor pains increase in frequency and intensity before a baby is born, so the "signs" that signal the end of this age will also become more prevalent and more powerful. Those signs include wars, violence, famines, earthquakes, pestilence, and more.

> [5] Jesus said to them: "Watch out that no one deceives you. [6] Many will come in my name, claiming, 'I am he,' and will deceive many. [7] When you hear of wars and rumors of wars, do not be alarmed. Such things must happen, but the end is still to come. [8] Nation will rise against nation, and kingdom against kingdom. There will be earthquakes in various places, and famines. These are the beginning of birth pains.
>
> MARK 13:5-8

Where do you see evidence of some of these signs in our world today? To what degree would you say that those signs are becoming more frequent and intense?

Read through the rest of Jesus' Olivet Discourse in Mark 13:9–37. What are the primary messages or themes that Jesus was communicating to his disciples?

PRAY | 10 MINUTES

Conclude this session by affirming the truth that God is a Savior by nature. Praise him for the ways that he has rescued you. Ask the Holy Spirit to give you clarity of mind and heart as you work through the rest of this session's material on the rapture and eternal rewards. Use the space below to write down any requests so that you and your group members can continue to pray about them in the week ahead.

NAME	REQUEST

PERSONAL STUDY

We have spent the first two sessions of this study laying the foundation for our exploration of the end times. God's original plan in the garden of Eden was for humanity to reign, and we *will* reign when God's kingdom is again established on earth. God made many promises (covenants) in Scripture that have yet to be fulfilled, and those covenants guide our understanding of history. Beyond those covenants, God has laid out a time line for history that reveals key events in the future. Many of those events point forward to a thousand-year period in the future called the millennium. In this study, we will look more closely at the "next" part of *what happens next*—namely, the rapture and the rewards we will receive at the judgment seat of Christ.

THE PEOPLE OF PARADISE

Where will I go when I die? This is a crucial query for each of us to ponder—and a great one for us to consider while we have the ability to ponder. It is also a question the church has been called on to answer for centuries. We have been given the gospel so that we can tell people with confidence that they will experience eternal life if they accept Jesus as their Savior.

But have we been giving the right response? Most people believe they will go to heaven when they die. This is true of both Christians and non-Christians. But that belief doesn't actually match up with what the Bible teaches.

What we call *heaven* is eternity—our eternal home. But as we'll see in the final session, we won't reach that eternal home until the "new heavens" and "new earth" have been established *after the* millennium. (Remember, the millennium will occur after the rapture and the tribulation.) No believers will reach their eternal heavenly home until after God has rendered his final judgments against all who reject him.

So, going back to the original question: *Where will I go when I die?* The answer is *Paradise.* Remember what Jesus told the thief on the cross next to him? "Truly I tell you, today you will be with me in paradise" (Luke 23:43). Paradise is where the souls of believers currently reside. It is where we will meet with Jesus—whether through our death on this earth or being "caught up" while we are still living by Jesus during the rapture.

Paradise is like heaven, but it's not our permanent home. In many ways, it is the front porch of heaven. It is wondrous and glorious because Jesus is there. Paul was referring to his own vision of Paradise when he wrote, "I know a man in Christ who fourteen years ago was caught up to the third heaven. . . . And I know that this man—whether in the body or apart from the body I do not know, but God knows—was caught up to paradise and heard inexpressible things, things that no one is permitted to tell" (2 Corinthians 12:2-4).

It is important to know that Paradise isn't some form of purgatory. It is not a place that we go to become worthy of entering into heaven. Rather, Paradise is the community of believers already experiencing a heavenly existence in the presence of God.

1. The concept of Paradise can be shocking to followers of Jesus who have only thought in terms of this world (earth) and the final world (heaven). How do you respond to this description of Paradise? What questions come to mind?

2. Read the story of Jesus and the criminals who hung on the crosses next to him in Luke 23:39–43. What request did the second criminal make? Remember that this was a man whose crimes had been severe enough for him to be convicted and crucified. What does this reveal about who can enter into Paradise?

Some teachers have proposed a transitional period of penance, a "holding tank" in which we are punished for our sins. This "purgatory" is the place where, for an undetermined length of time, we receive what our sins deserve so that we can rightly receive what God has prepared. Two problems derail this idea. First, none of us can endure what our sins deserve. Second, Jesus already has. The wages of sin is death, not purgatory (see Romans 6:23). The Bible also teaches that Jesus became our purgatory and took our punishment: "When he had brought about the purgation of sins, he took his seat at the right hand of Majesty on high" (Hebrews 1:3 NEB). Our purgatory occurred at Calvary when Jesus endured it for our sake.[9]

3. One definition of *purgatory* is "a place or state of punishment wherein . . . the souls of those who die in God's grace may make satisfaction for past sins and so become fit for heaven."[10] How would you describe the difference between purgatory and Paradise? Which of those concepts better matches what you have discovered about God's grace in Scripture?

4. Read Acts 7:54–60. One of the similarities between Paradise and heaven is that we will encounter the presence of God in each place. We will experience his majesty and love with no veil between us. How does Stephen's vision of Paradise support this claim? What excites you the most when you consider that future expansion of your relationship with God?

Who then is the one who condemns? No one. Christ Jesus who died—more than that, who was raised to life—is at the right hand of God and is also interceding for us.

ROMANS 8:34

Therefore, since we are surrounded by such a great cloud of witnesses, let us throw off everything that hinders and the sin that so easily entangles. And let us run with perseverance the race marked out for us, fixing our eyes on Jesus, the pioneer and perfecter of faith. For the joy set before him he endured the cross, scorning its shame, and sat down at the right hand of the throne of God.

HEBREWS 12:1–2

5. Jesus is currently present in Paradise, seated at the right hand of the Father. What is he doing there? He is interceding for us. Praying for us. But he is not the only one; we also have a "great cloud of witnesses" in Paradise who intercede for us—including our loved ones who have died before us. As you think back to your own loved ones who have passed, which of them can you envision praying for you right now? What are they praying for?

HOLY *HARPAZŌ*

There are several words that have become common in the language of Christianity but don't actually appear in the Bible. The word *Trinity* is a good example. Scripture never speaks directly of God existing as a Trinity, yet the pages of the Bible are filled with references to the Father, the Son, and the Holy Spirit in ways that help us understand that reality. One example is when Jesus told his disciples to baptize "in the name of the Father and of the Son and of the Holy Spirit" (Matthew 28:19).

The word *rapture* is another good example. You won't find that particular word used in the Bible, but you will certainly find the event. The best example comes from the following passage: "For the Lord himself will come down from heaven, with a loud command, with the voice of the archangel and with the trumpet call of God, and the dead in Christ will rise first. After that, we who are still alive and are left will be caught up together with them in the clouds to meet the Lord in the air. And so we will be with the Lord forever" (1 Thessalonians 4:16–17).

The phrase "caught up" in verse 17 comes from the Greek word *harpazō*.[11] It describes a mysterious miracle that will occur at some point in the future. At just the right moment, Jesus will step into our world and gather his people to himself. Paul makes it clear in verse 16 that "the dead in Christ will rise first." The body of every believer who has died will be resurrected and rejoined with their spirit in Paradise. "After that," Paul writes in verse 17, every believer who is alive will experience *harpazō*. They will be caught up to meet with Christ.

This means that there will be a generation of Christians who will not experience physical death. They will be alive one moment on earth and then alive the next in Paradise. Like Enoch and Elijah, they will enter the next phase of life through a doorway that does not include dying.

When will this occur? We don't know. As Jesus has said, "But about that day or hour no one knows, not even the angels in heaven, nor the Son, but only the Father" (Matthew 24:36). What we do know is that the rapture could occur at any moment. It could happen seven hundred years from now—or seven seconds from now. Therefore, we must be ready at all times for our Lord's return.

1. What (or who) are some of the sources of information that have formed your opinions about the rapture?

2. The sudden removal of every Christian during the rapture will be a shock to nations, governments, communities, and more. What might be some of the major consequences or reactions to the rapture in the days that follow?

Envisioning the rapture reminds me of a job I had during Christmas break in college. I worked in a machine shop. One of my tasks was to sweep the floor at the end of the day. My dustpan would be littered with trash, dirt, wood shavings, and assorted junk. The pile also included a random collection of nails, nuts, bolts, and screws. The machinists might need these. Separating the good stuff from the bad stuff was easy. Just hover a magnet over the trash. Every item that contained the same properties of the magnet would rise out of the box and attach to it. Everything else was left behind.

The rapture will have a similar effect. Jesus will appear in the sky, and all who share his nature—who house his Spirit, who have within them the presence of Christ—will be caught up by his magnetic presence to meet him in the air.[12]

3. Paul said to one congregation, "You, brothers and sisters, are not in darkness so that this day should surprise you like a thief" (1 Thessalonians 5:4). In terms of biblical prophecy, the rapture *could happen at any moment.* How should that reality influence your day-to-day life and routines?

4. Some feel the idea of the rapture is too fantastical to be taken literally. Yet the Bible reveals that God often works in ways that seem fantastical to us. Furthermore, we have examples in Scripture of people who left this world through

means other than physical death. Review the following passages and write down what they say about each person's departure.

Passage	How this person departed earth
Genesis 5:21–24	
2 Kings 2:11–12	
Acts 1:6–9[13]	

> [36] While they were still talking about this, Jesus himself stood among them and said to them, "Peace be with you."
>
> [37] They were startled and frightened, thinking they saw a ghost. [38] He said to them, "Why are you troubled, and why do doubts rise in your minds? [39] Look at my hands and my feet. It is I myself! Touch me and see; a ghost does not have flesh and bones, as you see I have."
>
> [40] When he had said this, he showed them his hands and feet. [41] And while they still did not believe it because of joy and amazement, he asked them, "Do you have anything here to eat?" [42] They gave him a piece of broiled fish, [43] and he took it and ate it in their presence.
>
> LUKE 24:36-43

5. Just as Jesus received a new body after his resurrection, so we will receive glorified bodies after the rapture. Those bodies will be physical yet devoid of the effects of sin. What are you looking forward to about your future glorified body?

CROWNED BY CHRIST

When it comes to *what happens next* in heaven's time line, the answer is the rapture. But what will happen after the rapture? The answer is the judgment seat of Christ.

Now, that may sound scary, but actually it's not. It's a wonderful moment. In Paradise, Jesus will gather his followers together from every era in the history of the world. In the midst of that great gathering, Jesus will reward his followers for the acts of service they performed during their earthly lives.

Paul wrote about this moment several times, including in this passage: "So we make it our goal to please him, whether we are at home in the body or away from it. For we must all appear before the judgment seat of Christ, so that each of us may receive what is due us for the things done while in the body, whether good or bad" (2 Corinthians 5:9-10).

The word that Paul uses to describe Jesus' judgment seat is *bēma.* In the ancient world, the *bēma* was the place where the judges sat during athletic competitions. The athletes stood in front of the *bēma* and received crowns from the judges based on their performance. Those crowns, also called "laurels," were typically woven from branches or vines.

In a similar way, the Bible speaks of several different crowns that followers of Jesus will receive at the judgment seat of Christ. These include the crown of self-control, the crown of influence, the crown of life, the crown of righteousness, and the crown of glory. Receiving these crowns will have nothing to do with our salvation—rather, they represent God's recognition for what we have achieved on behalf of his kingdom during our time spent on earth.

So, the question becomes, what does this mean for each of us as followers of Jesus? What should this compel us to do in our daily lives? In the words of Paul, "Do you not know that in a race all the runners run, but only one gets the prize? Run in such a way as to get the prize. Everyone who competes in the games goes into strict training. They do it to get a crown that will not last, but we do it to get a crown that will last forever" (1 Corinthians 9:24-25).

1. One of the premises of the Christian faith is that salvation is "not a result of works" (Ephesians 2:9 ESV). We cannot earn our way into heaven. Given this truth, what makes the judgment seat of Christ different from salvation being earned by works?

2. At the end of your life, you will receive a certain level of rewards (or crowns) that will be determined by what you did with that life. What comes to mind when you consider this? What emotions do you experience when you contemplate that future reality?

> [10] By the grace God has given me, I laid a foundation as a wise builder, and someone else is building on it. But each one should build with care. [11] For no one can lay any foundation other than the one already laid, which is Jesus Christ. [12] If anyone builds on this foundation using gold, silver, costly stones, wood, hay or straw, [13] their work will be shown for what it is, because the Day will bring it to light. It will be revealed with fire, and the fire will test the quality of each person's work. [14] If what has been built survives, the builder will receive a reward. [15] If it is burned up, the builder will suffer loss but yet will be saved—even though only as one escaping through the flames.
>
> 1 CORINTHIANS 3:10–15

3. Paul reveals that it is possible for followers of Jesus to waste the gifts they have been given and have nothing to show him at the end of their lives. What happens to those who build a foundation on anything other than the gospel of Christ? What does it mean that "the fire" will test the quality of every person's work?

4. What are some of the resources you've been given as a follower of Jesus? Where do you have opportunities to invest those resources in ways that will make an impact for eternity?

"Then the twenty-four elders bow down before the One who sits on the throne, and they worship him who lives forever and ever. They put their crowns down before the throne and say: 'You are worthy, our Lord and God, to receive glory and honor and power, because you made all things'" (Revelation 4:10–11 NCV).

Yes, there will come a day when you will be crowned. Your Maker will praise what you have done. He will bless you. But he will have hardly finished before you fall on your face and lay your crown at his feet. How gracious of him to give us a crown. For if he didn't, what would we have to give him? As joyfully as you receive it, you will surrender it. As freely as he gave it, you will offer it.[14]

5. The judgment seat of Christ will be an opportunity for all believers to offer their crowns to Christ. What opportunities do you have right now to show glory, reverence, and honor to Jesus? What might that look like in your present life here on earth?

CATCH UP AND READ AHEAD

Connect with a fellow group member and discuss some of the key insights from this session. Use any of the following prompts to help guide your discussion.

- What struck you as most interesting or surprising from this session? Why?
- Before this session, did you recognize that there is a difference between Paradise and heaven? How could you now describe the difference?
- Do you feel more nervous or excited when you contemplate the rapture as an *imminent* possibility in your future? Why do you feel that way?
- What do you learn about God's nature and character by studying the promise that followers of Jesus will be taken out of this world in the rapture?
- Is it right or wrong for us to perform good works here on earth because we desire a reward at the judgment seat of Christ? Explain your answer.

Use this time to go back and complete any of the study and reflection questions from previous days that you weren't able to finish. Make a note below of any revelations you've had and reflect on any growth or personal insights you've gained.

Read chapters 9–11 in *What Happens Next* before the next group gathering. Use the space below to make note of anything that stands out to you or encourages you.

WEEK 4

BEFORE GROUP MEETING	Read chapters 9–11 in *What Happens Next* Read the Welcome section (page 65)
GROUP MEETING	Discuss the Connect questions Watch the video teaching for session 4 Discuss the questions that follow as a group Do the closing exercise and pray (pages 65–70)
STUDY 1	Complete the personal study (pages 72–74)
STUDY 2	Complete the personal study (pages 75–77)
STUDY 3	Complete the personal study (pages 78–80)
CATCH UP AND READ AHEAD (BEFORE WEEK 5 GROUP MEETING)	Read chapters 12–13 in *What Happens Next* Complete any unfinished personal studies (page 81)

DESTINATION WEDDING

"The kingdom of heaven is like a king who prepared a wedding banquet for his son. He sent his servants to those who had been invited to the banquet to tell them to come, but they refused to come. Then he sent some more servants and said, 'Tell those who have been invited that I have prepared my dinner: . . . everything is ready. Come to the wedding banquet.'"

MATTHEW 22:2-4

HEAVEN'S
TIME LINE

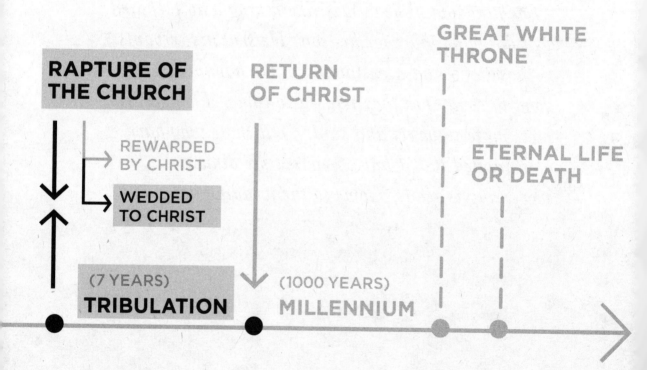

RAPTURE OF THE CHURCH

RETURN OF CHRIST

GREAT WHITE THRONE

REWARDED BY CHRIST

WEDDED TO CHRIST

ETERNAL LIFE OR DEATH

(7 YEARS) **TRIBULATION**

(1000 YEARS) MILLENNIUM

NOT TO SCALE

WELCOME | READ ON YOUR OWN

Juxtaposition is the practice of placing two things close together for the purpose of comparison. For instance, imagine a zoo creating an exhibit with a tiger in one space and a house cat next door. That would be an example of juxtaposition. We find another example of juxtaposition in Revelation 19.

The first event is the wedding feast of the Lamb, which takes place in Paradise after the rapture and the judgment seat of Christ. John recorded the following about that auspicious moment: "I heard what sounded like a great multitude, like the roar of rushing waters and like loud peals of thunder, shouting: 'Hallelujah! For our Lord God Almighty reigns. Let us rejoice and be glad and give him glory! For the wedding of the Lamb has come, and his bride has made herself ready'" (Revelation 19:6–7).

The picture painted in those verses is both wonderful and inconceivable. Jesus, the Lord of the universe, will unite himself with the members of the church from every age of human history. In spite of our sin and failures, God will unite himself with us.

So what is the juxtaposition? After the rapture, things will go very differently on earth. The removal of Christians will create a moral and spiritual void. The Antichrist will come onto the scene, and he will author seven years of chaos, including persecution of those who show signs of worshiping God. The wedding feast of the Lamb will be a celebration of intimate love. The tribulation will be a twisted carnival of rebellion and hate. Both events will precede the final conflict we call Armageddon.

CONNECT | 15 MINUTES

Get this session started by choosing one or both of the following questions to discuss together as a group:

- What is something that spoke to you in last week's personal study that you would like to share with the group?

— *or* —

- What are some specific kinds of suffering or persecution that cause an emotional reaction inside you?

WATCH | 20 MINUTES

Now watch the video for this session. Below is an outline of the key points covered during the teaching. Record any key concepts that stand out to you.

OUTLINE

I. The next event on God's calendar for history is known as the marriage feast of the Lamb.
   A. Several times in the New Testament, the church is referred to as the bride of Christ.
   B. In Revelation 19:7–8, the apostle John described the moment when Christ will officially claim his bride as part of a wedding ceremony in Paradise.
   C. The image of a wedding denotes unity and intimacy between Jesus and all Christians.

II. In the ancient world, weddings consisted of a private ceremony and a public celebration.
   A. The private ceremony between Jesus and his bride will take place in Paradise.
   B. The public celebration will take place on earth throughout the millennium.
   C. During ancient times, the groom paid money to the father of the bride. Jesus paid with his own life (his blood) so that we could eternally be with him.

III. Meanwhile, on the earth, nations and governments will be descending into chaos.
   A. The tribulation will begin at some point after the rapture occurs.
   B. People will turn away from God in huge numbers instead of turning to him.
   C. The Antichrist will step in to fill the leadership void caused by the departure of Christians throughout the world, and he will further push cultures away from God.

IV. John described many judgments and terrors that will occur during the tribulation.
   A. The "four horsemen of the apocalypse" that John described in Revelation 6:1–8 represent conquest, violence, famine, and death.
   B. The seven trumpet judgments that John described in Revelation 8:16–9:21 will add more calamity to the earth, including natural disasters.
   C. The tribulation will be unlike anything ever experienced before in human history.

V. Yet God will use even the circumstances of the tribulation to draw people to himself.
   A. A group of 144,000 Jewish evangelists will preach the gospel to the world, resulting in huge numbers of converts. This will be the finest hour for the Jewish people.
   B. The tribulation reminds us of the horrors of sin, the deception of Satan, and the grace of God in that he will rescue so many before it begins.
   C. Choose today to be in attendance at God's great "destination wedding"!

NOTES

DISCUSS | 35 MINUTES

Discuss what you just watched by answering the following questions.

1. Paul wrote to one group of believers that husbands are to love their wives "just as Christ loved the church and gave himself up for her" (Ephesians 5:25). What does the imagery of the church being the "bride of Christ" reveal about the relationship that God wants to have with each of us?

2. In John's vision, he heard the voice of a multitude shouting, "The wedding of the Lamb has come, and his bride has made herself ready" (Revelation 19:7). Why does the Bible describes the entrance of Christians into Paradise as a *wedding*? What is God saying about the type of union we will have in Paradise?

3. After the rapture, all the influence that followers of Jesus exerted will suddenly be removed from the world. Where do you currently see believers making a positive influence in society? What do you think the world will be like once that influence is removed?

4. Read aloud Revelation 6:1-17. Our culture typically associates the end of the world with war, famine, disease, and natural disasters. Much of that association comes from the judgments described in this passage. What do each of the four riders represent? What emotions do you experience as you read these verses?

5. Followers of Jesus will be taken into Paradise before the catastrophic events of the tribulation happen on earth. So why should Christians be concerned about the tribulation? Why does God spell out the facts of what will happen to people who do not accept the invitation of Christ?

RESPOND | 10 MINUTES

The tribulation will be a time of chaos and terror, but it will also be a time of salvation for a huge multitude of people. Consider what the apostle John saw during his vision:

> 9 After this I looked, and there before me was a great multitude that no one could count, from every nation, tribe, people and language, standing before the throne and before the Lamb. They were wearing white robes and were holding palm branches in their hands. 10 And they cried out in a loud voice:
> "Salvation belongs to our God, who sits on the throne, and to the Lamb.". . .
> 13 Then one of the elders asked me, "These in white robes—who are they, and where did they come from?"
> 14 I answered, "Sir, you know."
> And he said, "These are they who have come out of the great tribulation; they have washed their robes and made them white in the blood of the Lamb."
>
> REVELATION 7:9-10, 13-14

What can you learn about the "great multitude" from these verses? What can you learn from these verses about what life will be like during the tribulation?

The tribulation will be a last chance for evangelism in our world—but we have not yet reached it. What steps can you take this week to share the gospel with someone who needs to hear it?

PRAY | 10 MINUTES

Conclude this session by praying about the reality of suffering and persecution that exists in our world. Ask that God would give you and your group members eyes to see ways in which you can help ease any suffering in your community. Also pray that God would give you the opportunity to share the message of Jesus with those in need of the gospel. Use the space below to write down any requests so that you and your group members can continue to pray about them in the week ahead.

NAME   **REQUEST**

PERSONAL STUDY

In the previous session, you focused on two events that will happen *next* in God's time line: (1) the rapture of the church, and then (2) the judgment seat of Christ. Both of those events will only be experienced by believers. Meanwhile, those who were left behind on earth will be enduring a chaotic seven-year period known as the tribulation. However, in this study we will start by looking at the marriage supper of the Lamb, which will be a uniquely wonderful event for believers in Paradise. As you work through each of these exercises, be sure to write down your responses to the questions. (If you are engaging this study as part of a group, you will be given a few minutes to share your insights at the start of the next session.) If you are reading *What Happens Next* alongside this study, first review chapters 9–11 in the book.

BRIDE AND GROOM

In our culture, we are used to romantic relationships being a two-way street. This includes the initial dating or courtship phase. Both the man and the woman actively pursue one another. Both evaluate each another. Both have a choice when it comes to proceeding in the relationship or ending it. Both the man and the woman walk down the aisle as equal partners when the big day comes.

However, this is not the case when it come to the "courtship" between Jesus and his bride, which is the church. When it comes to our relationship with Christ, we have nothing to give. We have nothing to offer him that he does not already possess. He is holy and righteous; we are filthy and unrighteous. He is all-powerful and all-knowing, which means he is deeply aware of our faults. We carry nothing of worth and are bogged down by our sin.

If there were ever to be a connection between humanity and God, it was up to God to make it happen. Incredibly, this is exactly what he did! As John wrote, "This is love: not that we loved God, but that he loved us and sent his Son as an atoning sacrifice for our sins" (1 John 4:10).

Paul added, "You see, at just the right time, when we were still powerless, Christ died for the ungodly. Very rarely will anyone die for a righteous person, though for a good person someone might possibly dare to die. But God demonstrates his own love for us in this: While we were still sinners, Christ died for us" (Romans 5:6–8).

Jesus' love for us applies not only to our present but also to our future—to our eternity with him. In the Jewish world of Jesus' day, it was expected for a groom to build a home for himself and his beloved on his father's property. Once the engagement was official, the groom would return home and immediately get to work building their future home.

Likewise, Jesus has told us, "My Father's house has many rooms; if that were not so, would I have told you that I am going there to prepare a place for you? And if I go and prepare a place for you, I will come back and take you to be with me that you also may be where I am" (John 14:2–3).

1. Weddings cause mixed reactions among people today. Think back to your experiences with weddings (both as a guest and a participant). What are some of the biggest emotions or experiences that you associate with those events?

2. The prophet Isaiah wrote, "All of us have become like one who is unclean, and all our righteous acts are like filthy rags" (Isaiah 64:6). Think for a moment about the reality that you have nothing to offer Jesus as your groom. In many ways, the relationship between you and Christ is one-sided. What are some suitable ways for you to respond to that reality?

> 25 Husbands, love your wives, just as Christ loved the church and gave himself up for her 26 to make her holy, cleansing her by the washing with water through the word, 27 and to present her to himself as a radiant church, without stain or wrinkle or any other blemish, but holy and blameless. 28 In this same way, husbands ought to love their wives as their own bodies. He who loves his wife loves himself. 29 After all, no one ever hated their own body, but they feed and care for their body, just as Christ does the church—30 for we are members of his body. 31 "For this reason a man will leave his father and mother and be united to his wife, and the two will become one flesh." 32 This is a profound mystery—but I am talking about Christ and the church.
>
> EPHESIANS 5:25-32

3. Circle any words in the verses above that describe the church. Because you are part of the church, those words describe you as well. What obstacles, if any, are hindering your ability to believe that Jesus loves you in this way—that he treasures you and approves of you?

4. Every marriage relationship has roles. One spouse is responsible for certain things, while the other takes on other responsibilities. In the relationship between Christ and his church, what responsibilities do we carry? How do we participate in our relationship with God?

Never has there been, never will there be, a wedding like our wedding in heaven. Angels will hover above us. Our praise will well up within us. We will witness the end of this age and the beginning of the next. Sin and death? No more. Tears and fears? No more. Disease and debt, guilt and regret, addictions and afflictions, wars and rage? No more. Not in God's house.

What a wedding. Contemplate it. Ponder it. Set your heart upon it. Let your wedding day define the way you live on this day.

You are engaged, set apart, called out, a holy bride. You've already given your hand to be married. Don't settle for one-night stands in sleazy motels. You belong to him. Moreover, he wants to see you more than you want to see him. He has set his sights on you. He died to save you, and he lives to receive you. "He can bring you before his glory without any wrong in you and can give you great joy" (Jude 24 NCV).[15]

5. Read Jude 1:17–23. How do you stay motivated to continue building yourself up "in your most holy faith" as you look toward this great wedding day with Christ? What can you do to snatch those who need Jesus "from the fire" so they can experience this day as well?

THE REALITY OF CONSEQUENCES

Judgment is a word that most people in the church don't like. It makes us feel uncomfortable. It puts us on edge. We shake our heads not only at the thought of God being aware of who we are and judging what we do as individuals but also of God extending his judgment against whole groups of people—even against the people of the entire world.

Even so, judgment is a reality in God's Word, which means it is—and will be—a reality in our world. Again and again in Scripture, we read about God willingly taking up the mantle of "judge" over the cosmos. As one psalmist wrote, "Rise up, Judge of the earth; pay back to the proud what they deserve" (Psalm 94:2). Despite our awkwardness, God is comfortable in his role as a judge. Why? Because judgment is part of his nature.

Paul understood this truth about God and wrote clearly on the subject: "But because of your stubbornness and your unrepentant heart, you are storing up wrath against yourself for the day of God's wrath, when his righteous judgment will be revealed. God 'will repay each person according to what they have done.' To those who by persistence in doing good seek glory, honor and immortality, he will give eternal life. But for those who are self-seeking and who reject the truth and follow evil, there will be wrath and anger" (Romans 2:5–8).

Even so, God has been patient. He has withheld the full force of his judgment for thousands of years, deeply desiring that all who desire to place themselves under his grace have the opportunity to do so. Peter expressed this profound truth when he wrote, "The Lord is not slow in keeping his promise, as some understand slowness. Instead he is patient with you, not wanting anyone to perish, but everyone to come to repentance" (2 Peter 3:9).

One day, however, God's patience will end, and judgment will begin. God will pour out his wrath on sin, evil, and rebellion. He will pour out his wrath on our fallen world—one filled with sinful and fallen people. And none will escape the consequences of their actions.

1. Solomon wrote, "God will bring into judgment both the righteous and the wicked, for there will be a time for every activity, a time to judge every deed" (Ecclesiastes 3:17). How would you describe what it means for God to execute his judgment against people?

2. Judgment is common in our world today. Parents exercise judgment in their households. So do bosses, teachers, coaches, and—of course—judges. Why do you think judgment is such a necessary part our society? Why is judgment a necessary part of God's plan for history?

³ Don't let anyone deceive you in any way, for that day will not come until the rebellion occurs and the man of lawlessness is revealed, the man doomed to destruction. ⁴ He will oppose and will exalt himself over everything that is called God or is worshiped, so that he sets himself up in God's temple, proclaiming himself to be God.

⁵ Don't you remember that when I was with you I used to tell you these things? ⁶ And now you know what is holding him back, so that he may be revealed at the proper time. ⁷ For the secret power of lawlessness is already at work; but the one who now holds it back will continue to do so till he is taken out of the way. ⁸ And then the lawless one will be revealed, whom the Lord Jesus will overthrow with the breath of his mouth and destroy by the splendor of his coming. ⁹ The coming of the lawless one will be in accordance with how Satan works. He will use all sorts of displays of power through signs and wonders that serve the lie, ¹⁰ and all the ways that wickedness deceives those who are perishing. They perish because they refused to love the truth and so be saved.

2 THESSALONIANS 2:3–10

3. Many people in Thessalonica were believing a false rumor that the day of the Lord had already occurred. Paul wrote these words to correct them and explain what would truly happen during the time of God's judgment of the world. What can we learn about the tribulation based on Paul's description in this passage?

4. Paul makes frequent references in 2 Thessalonians 2:3–10 to a "man of lawlessness" who will be revealed at some time in the future. We know from other places in Scripture that Paul was referring to the Antichrist. What does Paul say is "holding him back" from appearing on the scene (see also 2 Peter 3:9)? What will happen when the Antichrist does appear?

Though terrible, the tribulation is instructive. It reminds us that *God hates sin*. He hates what turns people away from him and into violent, depraved, self-centered creatures. It reminds us that *Satan is a deceiver*. He's lied since the beginning and will lie until the end. He's allergic to the truth. He knows how to dazzle with the promise of peace and the appearance of power. He knows how to control people so they will worship him, not God. For a time during the tribulation, the earthbound will do just that.

There is another reason for understanding the tribulation. *You might experience it*. This is not as far-fetched as you might think. Are you keeping Christ at arm's length? If so, God is spelling out the facts. He is describing the consequences. Love does this. Love tells you where the road of disobedience takes you.[16]

5. It sounds strange, but God's judgment is ultimately an expression of his love. Take a moment to think through your recent circumstances and experiences. In what ways have you been keeping Christ at arm's length or resisting his love and his will?

THE LAMB TAKES THE SCROLL

The Bible has a lot to say about what people will experience during the seven years of chaos we call the tribulation. There are many verses and passages that point forward to that period of terror and violence and persecution. We don't have a lot of specifics—we don't have a lot of details about what will happen in people's everyday lives during the tribulation—but we do have a lot of information that helps us understand the distressing nature of those times.

The book of Revelation offers the most comprehensive look at what life might be like during the tribulation. In one scene, John describes the heavenly event that will set the stage for earthly tribulation: "Then I saw in the right hand of him who sat on the throne a scroll with writing on both sides and sealed with seven seals. And I saw a mighty angel proclaiming in a loud voice, 'Who is worthy to break the seals and open the scroll?' But no one in heaven or on earth or under the earth could open the scroll or even look inside it. I wept and wept because no one was found who was worthy to open the scroll or look inside. Then one of the elders said to me, 'Do not weep! See, the Lion of the tribe of Judah, the Root of David, has triumphed. He is able to open the scroll and its seven seals'" (Revelation 5:1–5).

In the first century, the only document sealed with seven seals was a last will and testament.[17] This means that John's original readers would have recognized this particular scroll as an inheritance. The mighty angel that John sees in his vision was thus seeking someone worthy to inherit the world—to be king over the universe. When John learned that *no one worthy was found,* he wept at the thought of a kingless cosmos . . . that there was no one with authority to take control.

But then Jesus enters the stage in the form of a lamb (see verse 6). He is the King! He proved himself worthy on the cross. As John writes, "He went and took the scroll from the right hand of him who sat on the throne" (verse 7). When Jesus receives his rightful inheritance, the residents of Paradise rejoice. But the same is not true on the earth. There, Satan and the rebels tremble, because they understand the King is coming to take back his kingdom and establish his throne.

1. Take a moment to skim through Revelation 5 and 6. What images strike you as most interesting from those chapters? What is the theme communicated by John once Jesus accepts his inheritance and opens the seals?

> ⁶ Then the seven angels who had the seven trumpets prepared to sound them.
>
> ⁷ The first angel sounded his trumpet, and there came hail and fire mixed with blood, and it was hurled down on the earth. A third of the earth was burned up, a third of the trees were burned up, and all the green grass was burned up.
>
> ⁸ The second angel sounded his trumpet, and something like a huge mountain, all ablaze, was thrown into the sea. A third of the sea turned into blood, ⁹ a third of the living creatures in the sea died, and a third of the ships were destroyed.
>
> ¹⁰ The third angel sounded his trumpet, and a great star, blazing like a torch, fell from the sky on a third of the rivers and on the springs of water—¹¹ the name of the star is Wormwood. A third of the waters turned bitter, and many people died from the waters that had become bitter.
>
> ¹² The fourth angel sounded his trumpet, and a third of the sun was struck, a third of the moon, and a third of the stars, so that a third of them turned dark. A third of the day was without light, and also a third of the night.
>
> REVELATION 8:6–12

2. The above verses represent one example of the kinds of judgments that God will implement during the tribulation. What do you notice about the first three trumpet judgments as they relate to the land, seas, and rivers on earth? What part of God's creation is he undoing with the fourth trumpet judgment?

The judgments mentioned in the book of Revelation are described in highly visual and highly symbolic language. ("A third of the earth was burned up." "A third of the sun was struck.") In your mind, is it more helpful or distracting to parse through the details of those verses in order to determine what specifically might happen during the tribulation? Explain your answer.

3. John describes the appointment of 144,000 Jewish evangelists in Revelation 7:1–8 who will zealously spread the gospel during the tribulation. Imagine for a moment that you were one of those evangelists. How would you point people to the gospel during such a chaotic time?

Who are these servants? . . . John offered two key details about these servants of God. They will be Jewish, and they will be "sealed"; that is, they will be marked, identified as God's chosen ones. Later John tells us the seal means having Jesus' "name and his Father's name written on their foreheads" (Revelation 14:1 NLT). . . . This will be a crack battalion of God's servants. Satan will throw his fire and brimstone at them, but they will not be destroyed. Invincible and unassailable. Nor will their work be futile. The description of the 144,000 is followed by the appearance of an innumerable multitude, implying that the work of these Jews will result in a massive harvest of souls.[18]

4. Look specifically at Revelation 7:9. Who is represented in the multitude around God's throne? What does this say about who is invited to join his kingdom?

CATCH UP AND READ AHEAD

Connect with a fellow group member and discuss some of the key insights from this session. Use any of the following prompts to help guide your discussion.

- Personally, how do you respond to the idea of being united with Jesus as part of his "bride"? What does that mean to you?
- Do you believe you are worthy to be wanted by Jesus? Explain.
- Why is it necessary for judgment to be part of God's nature and character?
- What surprised you the most in reading about the tribulation as described in the book of Revelation? Why did it impact you in that way?
- Who in your life is in danger of experiencing the tribulation? What possible steps can you take today to help them avoid that path?

Use this time to go back and complete any of the study and reflection questions from previous days that you weren't able to finish. Make a note below of any revelations you've had and reflect on any growth or personal insights you've gained.

Read chapters 12–13 in *What Happens Next* before the next group gathering. Use the space below to make note of anything that stands out to you or encourages you.

WEEK 5

BEFORE GROUP MEETING	Read chapters 12-13 in *What Happens Next* Read the Welcome section (page 85)
GROUP MEETING	Discuss the Connect questions Watch the video teaching for session 5 Discuss the questions that follow as a group Do the closing exercise and pray (pages 85-90)
STUDY 1	Complete the personal study (pages 92-94)
STUDY 2	Complete the personal study (pages 95-97)
STUDY 3	Complete the personal study (pages 98-100)
CATCH UP AND READ AHEAD (BEFORE WEEK 6 GROUP MEETING)	Read chapters 14-16 in *What Happens Next* Complete any unfinished personal studies (page 101)

GOD WILL HAVE HIS GARDEN

"Never again will there be in it an infant who lives but a few days, or an old man who does not live out his years; the one who dies at a hundred will be thought a mere child; the one who fails to reach a hundred will be considered accursed. They will build houses and dwell in them; they will plant vineyards and eat their fruit."

ISAIAH 65:20-21

HEAVEN'S
TIME LINE

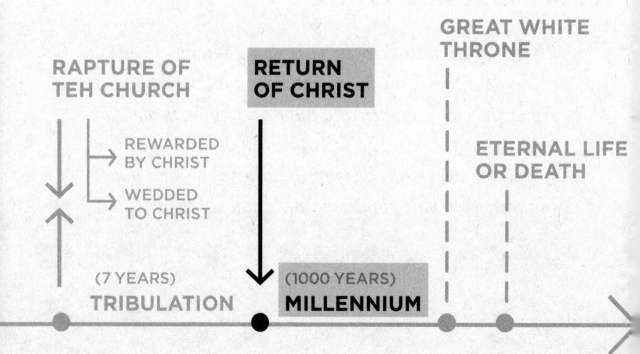

RAPTURE OF
TEH CHURCH

RETURN
OF CHRIST

GREAT WHITE
THRONE

REWARDED
BY CHRIST

WEDDED
TO CHRIST

ETERNAL LIFE
OR DEATH

(7 YEARS)
TRIBULATION

(1000 YEARS)
MILLENNIUM

NOT TO SCALE

WELCOME | READ ON YOUR OWN

We can all agree there are a lot of things wrong with our world today. We hear stories of wars, conflicts, and strife everywhere. We read accounts of people engaging in acts of hate, selfishness, and greed. We learn of loved ones suffering with depression, anxiety, and other afflictions. We all understand at a deep level that the way things *are* do not line up with the way things are *supposed to be.*

This is why the millennium is such a critical part of God's plan for history. The term *millennium* simply means a period of one thousand years. However, when we use it in reference to the end times, it speaks of a specific one-thousand year reign of Christ. For ten glorious centuries, humanity will get to experience what life on earth was always supposed to be like. We will get to see God's plans for this world and for all who inhabit it. Just about everything currently wrong with our society will be removed, and just about everything right will be amplified to an incredible degree.

We referred to the millennium in a previous session when we spoke of the different ways that people tend to interpret Scripture when it comes to God's plan for the future. Now it's time to take a deeper look at what the millennium will be and what we will experience during those thousand years. But first, it is important for us to remember that the millennium will only begin once the tribulation has ended. And the tribulation won't end until the rightful King returns to this world and claims his throne. Scholars often describe that event as the second coming of Christ. So let's dig into both of those themes as we continue our exploration of the end times.

CONNECT | 15 MINUTES

Get this session started by choosing one or both of the following questions to discuss together as a group:

- What is something that spoke to you in last week's personal study that you would like to share with the group?

— *or* —

- Think back to the best vacation you've ever taken. What did you enjoy most about that experience? What would you change if you could do it all again?

WATCH | 20 MINUTES

Now watch the video for this session. Below is an outline of the key points covered during the teaching. Record any key concepts that stand out to you.

OUTLINE

I. The second coming of Christ is the central focus of prophecy and a dominating theme throughout the pages of Scripture.
   A. Much of the tension we see in the Bible—and the tension we feel in our world—points forward to a coming confrontation between Jesus and Satan.
   B. The second coming is referenced more than three hundred times throughout the Bible, which is an average of once every twenty-five verses.[19]
   C. Jesus himself described his return to earth (see Matthew 24:30–31).

II. The apostle John was given a vision of the second coming (see Revelation 19:11–13).
   A. Jesus returns on a white stallion, which first-century readers would have associated with a conquering king who returned from battle riding a white horse.
   B. Jesus wears many crowns. In ancient times, when a king conquered an enemy, he would wear the crown of the defeated king.
   C. The chain of command is clear: Jesus is in charge and rules and reigns over everything.

III. The image that John presented of Jesus is of a mighty warrior (see Revelation 19:15).
   A. The armies of earth will gather on the fields of Armageddon to war against Christ.
   B. These are bad-to-the-bone rebels who choose Satan over salvation.
   C. The King has come to set them straight. Jesus defeats them all in the battle, and then the beast and false prophet are thrown in the lake of fire.

IV. The golden season called the millennium will begin immediately after the tribulation ends.
   A. Satan will be removed from the world and bound for a thousand years.
   B. Jesus will be enthroned in Jerusalem and will reign for a thousand years.
   C. *All* believers will join together on earth during the millennium and will reign with Christ.

V. The millennium will be as close to Utopia as we will ever get on this planet.
   A. Nature will return to a state of harmony (see Isaiah 11:6).
   B. There will be no more war or disease (see Isaiah 2:4; 65:20).
   C. God will honor the covenants. His children will again rule over creation.

NOTES

DISCUSS | 35 MINUTES

Discuss what you just watched by answering the following questions.

1. The author of Hebrews wrote, "So Christ, having been offered once to bear the sins of many, will appear a second time, not to deal with sin but to save those who are eagerly waiting for him" (Hebrews 9:28 ESV). What will be the purpose of the second coming? Why is Jesus' return good news for his faithful followers?

2. Read aloud Revelation 19:11–21. How does John's depiction of the second coming match up with your image of it? What is the same and what is different? What are some of the primary themes that John communicates in his vision?

3. What is the significance of Jesus wearing many crowns and riding on a white horse? What would first-century readers have associated with these images?

4. The tribulation will be seven years of chaos, terror, and persecution. The second coming will be an instant in which God destroys those who continue to rebel against him. What are some of the possible reasons as to why people will reject Jesus even to the end?

5. Ask someone to read aloud Revelation 20:1–6. Jesus' millennial kingdom will be unlike anything that humans have ever before experienced on this planet. Satan will finally be out of the picture for a time. What stands out to you the most in John's description of this millennial kingdom? What are you looking forward to most about those thousand years?

RESPOND | 10 MINUTES

In a previous session, we discussed how the prophet Daniel received information about end-times events, including the millennium. In one instance, while he was interpreting a dream for King Nebuchadnezzar of Babylon, he offered this description of Jesus' millennial kingdom:

> [44] "The God of heaven will set up a kingdom that will never be destroyed, nor will it be left to another people. It will crush all those kingdoms and bring them to an end, but it will itself endure forever. [45] This is the meaning of the vision of the rock cut out of a mountain, but not by human hands—a rock that broke the iron, the bronze, the clay, the silver and the gold to pieces.
>
> "The great God has shown the king what will take place in the future. The dream is true and its interpretation is trustworthy."
>
> DANIEL 2:44–45

Read through the full account of Nebuchadnezzar's dream and Daniel's interpretation of it in verses 29–45. What was the central message that God wanted to communicate through this dream? How does that message apply to people today?

Sometimes, we may understand the "nuts and bolts" of biblical prophecy without actually dealing with the reality in terms of our own lives. Do that now. If you believe the millennium is coming, how will that belief shape and impact your life today?

PRAY | 10 MINUTES

Conclude this session by expressing your trust in Jesus. Declare your belief that he has control over all things—even when the world and your life feel out of control. Affirm that he has the ultimately authority over Satan and all of his demonic forces. Praise him for the wonders he will produce in the future, including his millennial kingdom. Use the space below to write down any requests so that you and your group members can continue to pray about them in the week ahead.

NAME   **REQUEST**

PERSONAL STUDY

In the previous session, you saw the powerful juxtaposition of two future events: (1) the wedding feast of the Lamb, which will take place in Paradise; and (2) the tribulation, which will occur on earth after the rapture. In this session, you explored the next two events in heaven's time line: (1) the second coming of Jesus; and (2) the millennium, which will be a thousand years of peace, prosperity, and worship, the likes of which our world has never seen. As you work through each of these exercises, be sure to write down your responses to the questions. (If you are engaging this study as part of a group, you will be given a few minutes to share your insights at the start of the next session.) If you are reading *What Happens Next* alongside this study, first review the introduction and chapters 12–13 of the book.

THE LAMB WHO IS KING

Most of us understand Jesus best as the Lamb of God. (Well, perhaps not visually, given that picturing Jesus as a lamb can be a bit of a strange image.) But we understand Jesus to be the Son of God who died on our behalf so that our sins could be forgiven and we could receive salvation. We see Jesus as "the Lamb of God . . . who takes away the sin of the world" (John 1:29).

The apostle John maintained this imagery when he was describing Jesus in the throne room of heaven. He wrote, "Then I saw a Lamb, looking as if it had been slain, standing at the center of the throne, encircled by the four living creatures and the elders. The Lamb had seven horns and seven eyes, which are the seven spirits of God sent out into all the earth. He went and took the scroll from the right hand of him who sat on the throne" (Revelation 5:6–7).

So, yes, Jesus is the Lamb of God. In the words of one ancient prophet, "We all, like sheep, have gone astray, each of us has turned to our own way; and the Lord has laid on him the iniquity of us all. He was oppressed and afflicted, yet he did not open his mouth; he was led like a lamb to the slaughter, and as a sheep before its shearers is silent, so he did not open his mouth" (Isaiah 53:6–7).

But Jesus is also much more. According to John, Jesus is "the Lion of the tribe of Judah" and "the Root of David" (Revelation 5:5). In other words, there is a kingly cast to Christ. He comes from royal blood both in heaven and on earth. He may have allowed himself to be nailed to the cross as a suffering servant, but he rose again in glory, ascended to heaven in glory—and he will return to earth in mighty splendor as the King of kings and Lord of lords.

This is the Jesus that John saw in his vision of the second coming. He will return to our world in absolute victory—and he will appear wearing many crowns. Again, in the words of John: "I saw heaven standing open and there before me was a white horse, whose rider is called Faithful and True. With justice he judges and wages war. His eyes are like blazing fire, and on his head are many crowns. He has a name written on him that no one knows but he himself. He is dressed in a robe dipped in blood, and his name is the Word of God" (Revelation 19:11–13).

1. Read John 18:33–37. How did Jesus respond when Pilate asked if he was "the king of the Jews"? How did Jesus describe his kingdom to Pilate?

> 27 "For as lightning that comes from the east is visible even in the west, so will be the coming of the Son of Man. 28 Wherever there is a carcass, there the vultures will gather.
>
> 29 "Immediately after the distress of those days 'the sun will be darkened, and the moon will not give its light; the stars will fall from the sky, and the heavenly bodies will be shaken.'
>
> 30 "Then will appear the sign of the Son of Man in heaven. And then all the peoples of the earth will mourn when they see the Son of Man coming on the clouds of heaven, with power and great glory. 31 And he will send his angels with a loud trumpet call, and they will gather his elect from the four winds, from one end of the heavens to the other."
>
> MATTHEW 24:27–31

2. Jesus spoke these words to his disciples shortly before his arrest. How did Jesus describe the events leading up to his return? What will happen at his return?

3. Look again at John's description of Jesus' second coming in Revelation 19:11–21. What can you say for certain about Christ's triumphant return to this world? What is the emotional tone communicated by that passage and the verses you read in Matthew 24:27–31?

Christ's second advent will be unlike his first. The first coming was all about salvation. The second is all about coronation. In his first coming, Jesus Christ came to seek and save. In his second, he will come to rule and reign. In Jesus' first advent, he was falsely judged by evil men. In his second, he will rightly judge evil men. When he first came, his eyes wept at the tomb of Lazarus. When he reappears, his eyes will blaze with fire. Soldiers gave Jesus a crown of thorns. Christ will descend wearing all the crowns of history. People mocked him on his first advent. All will bow before him upon his second. "At the name of Jesus every knee shall bow in heaven and on earth and under the earth, and every tongue shall confess that Jesus Christ is Lord, to the glory of God the Father" (Philippians 2:10–11 TLB).[20]

4. Think of the leaders who are guiding our world today—heads of nations, government officials, CEOs of powerful corporations, and others. How do you expect Jesus to be different and behave differently from those world leaders?

5. "Jesus Christ is Lord" (Philippians 2:11 TLB). It's one thing to accept that Jesus is sovereign over the universe and will one day rule as king over the earth. It's another thing to recognize him as the king of *your life.* What does Jesus' kingdom mean for you personally?

A WORLD IN CRISIS

The prophet Isaiah wrote, "The earth is defiled by its people; they have disobeyed the laws, violated the statutes and broken the everlasting covenant. Therefore a curse consumes the earth; its people must bear their guilt." (Isaiah 24:5–6). We all inherently know that things are bad in this world. We know that things are off the mark in terms of God's orginal plan for creating.

But *why*? Why is everything so messed up?

One reason is because *Satan is on the prowl*. The devil has a stranglehold on the globe, and boy can he squeeze. Peter warned us to "be alert and of sober mind. Your enemy the devil prowls around like a roaring lion looking for someone to devour" (1 Peter 5:8). Jesus said the devil "was a murderer from the beginning, not holding to the truth, for there is no truth in him. When he lies, he speaks his native language, for he is a liar and the father of lies" (John 8:44).

A second reason our world is a mess is because *Jesus is unwelcome*. Certainly, there have been places in history that could be legitimately considered "Christian nations"—regions where a majority of the people worshiped Christ. But such places are few and far between today. Instead, most people in our modern world want nothing to do with a divine king. They prefer to manage their own lives, which is one of the reasons those lives become so troublesome.

A third reason our world is a mess is because we have been plagued with *unrighteous rulers*. Are there genuinely good and moral leaders in our world today? Absolutely. But for every decent person in authority, we can find dozens of others who are focused on corruption, self-interest, and doing whatever they can possibly do to gain the next rung on the ladder.

Incidentally, it was these kinds of leaders who spoiled the promise of ancient Israel. The prophet Micah said of them, "You leaders of Jacob, you rulers of Israel, who despise justice and distort all that is right. . . . Because of you, Zion will be plowed like a field, Jerusalem will become a heap of rubble, the temple hill a mound overgrown with thickets" (Micah 3:9, 12).

1. The influence of Satan on our world causes a lot of pain, suffering, confusion, and doubt. Based on your experience, what are some of the ways that Satan operates in our world? How have you recently been hurt or led astray by his influence?

[10] Finally, be strong in the Lord and in his mighty power. [11] Put on the full armor of God, so that you can take your stand against the devil's schemes. [12] For our struggle is not against flesh and blood, but against the rulers, against the authorities, against the powers of this dark world and against the spiritual forces of evil in the heavenly realms. [13] Therefore put on the full armor of God, so that when the day of evil comes, you may be able to stand your ground, and after you have done everything, to stand. [14] Stand firm then, with the belt of truth buckled around your waist, with the breastplate of righteousness in place, [15] and with your feet fitted with the readiness that comes from the gospel of peace. [16] In addition to all this, take up the shield of faith, with which you can extinguish all the flaming arrows of the evil one. [17] Take the helmet of salvation and the sword of the Spirit, which is the word of God.

EPHESIANS 6:10–17

2. Paul offers some helpful advice in this passage for mitigating Satan's influence in our lives—and even for deflecting his attacks against us. What does it look like on a practical level to "put on the full armor of God"? How does that work?

3. Jesus has become more and more unwelcome in our world today—especially in many Western societies. According to one survey, the percentage of those in America who call themselves Christians has declined from 90 percent in 1972 to 64 percent today.[21] What are some of the ways that you have seen the culture pressure you to think less of Jesus—and even reject him?

People want the benefits of Jesus. They want kindness, inclusion, forgiveness; they want the blessings of Christ's kingdom. But a king? An absolute authority? One who has the final say on our lives? That's another matter. . . . Christ, in other words, is rarely consulted. His words are irrelevant to most people. Jesus is unheard of in our homes, schools, even churches. As it stands, our world is a kingless kingdom.[22]

4. Read Matthew 7:21–23. What does Jesus say about those who call him "Lord" but do not show through their actions that he is truly the lord over their lives? What are some practical ways that you submit to Christ and seek to do his will?

5. The world today is unfortunately plagued with many unrighteous rulers. These "leaders" include not only politicians but also celebrities and others who wield a great deal of influence over people's lives. When have you personally felt let down or betrayed by one such leader?

RIGHT-SIDE UP ONCE MORE

There is an old phrase that used to be quite common in church circles: "This too shall pass." Saying it today feels a little dated. Maybe a little corny. Yet the phrase still carries a whole lot of truth. No matter how rough our world may seem at the moment, we can know for sure that it will not stay that way forever. The millennium is coming—a time when all that currently ails us will be removed or made right. Therefore, "This too shall pass."

One reason the millennium will be so wonderful is that Satan's influence will be completely removed from our world. The apostle John saw that removal in his vision on the island of Patmos: "And I saw an angel coming down out of heaven, having the key to the Abyss and holding in his hand a great chain. He seized the dragon, that ancient serpent, who is the devil, or Satan, and bound him for a thousand years" (Revelation 20:1–2).

Not only that, but Jesus will be welcomed wholeheartedly throughout this golden age. In fact, he will be more than just welcomed—he will also be *enthroned.* He will sit on the throne of his ancestor David in Jerusalem (see Psalm 132:11). People will flock from all over the world to see Jesus on that throne . . . to speak with him and interact with him face-to-face. Christ will be worshiped and celebrated in every way as our rightful and righteous king.

Speaking of which, we will no longer have to deal with unrighteous rulers during the millennium. Christ himself will be king, and he will reign with justice and mercy. We will also take up the mantle of leadership in the millennium. As John writes, "I saw thrones on which were seated those who had been given authority to judge. . . . They came to life and reigned with Christ a thousand years" (Revelation 20:4). Paul alluded to this reality as well: "Do you not know that the Lord's people will judge the world?" (1 Corinthians 6:2).

In short, the millennium will be a time when Satan is removed, Jesus is lifted high, and all the saints will participate in the governance of the world. They will lead alongside Christ with righteousness. What was upside down will finally be set right-side up once more.

1. Satan and his forces will be locked away during the millennium. What are some ways that your life might have been different if you had been spared the influence and attacks of Satan?

8 "Tell my servant David, 'This is what the LORD Almighty says: I took you from the pasture, from tending the flock, and appointed you ruler over my people Israel. 9 I have been with you wherever you have gone, and I have cut off all your enemies from before you. Now I will make your name great, like the names of the greatest men on earth. 10 And I will provide a place for my people Israel and will plant them so that they can have a home of their own and no longer be disturbed. Wicked people will not oppress them anymore, as they did at the beginning 11 and have done ever since the time I appointed leaders over my people Israel. I will also give you rest from all your enemies.

"'The LORD declares to you that the LORD himself will establish a house for you: 12 When your days are over and you rest with your ancestors, I will raise up your offspring to succeed you, your own flesh and blood, and I will establish his kingdom. 13 He is the one who will build a house for my Name, and I will establish the throne of his kingdom forever. 14 I will be his father, and he will be my son. When he does wrong, I will punish him with a rod wielded by men, with floggings inflicted by human hands. 15 But my love will never be taken away from him, as I took it away from Saul, whom I removed from before you. 16 Your house and your kingdom will endure forever before me; your throne will be established forever.'"

2 SAMUEL 7:8–16

2. This passage is from a prophecy spoken to King David through the prophet Nathan. Which elements of this prophecy connect directly with David's life? Which elements point forward to the millennium?

3. Jesus is largely unwelcome in our world today, but he will be worshiped during the millennium. Read Psalm 99:1-5. What role does worshiping God play in your life? Why do you think God commands his people to exalt him and worship him?

4. John states that not only will Jesus physically reign on the earth during the millennium but that also we will rule alongside him (see Revelation 20:4-5). How does it make you feel when you consider this truth? What are some of the gifts and talents that you use in your life today that might make you an asset during this coming golden age?

This world, so upside down, will be right side up. People who were rejected in this life will be respected in the next. In this age they were enslaved and sold. In the next they will rule and reign. In this age they were handicapped and sick; in the next they will serve with perfected, glorified bodies. Billions have been victims of cruel tyrants; in the next age they themselves will rule with righteousness. In this life they were aborted and discarded, considered an inconvenience; in the next they will be rewarded and consulted. They will serve in the presence of Jesus.[23]

5. The millennium will not be heaven, but it will be the closest thing that humanity has experienced to heaven since the garden of Eden. Look back at Genesis 2:4-25. What are some similarities between the garden and the golden age? What are some differences?

CATCH UP AND READ AHEAD

Connect with a fellow group member and discuss some of the key insights from this session. Use any of the following prompts to help guide your discussion.

- Why is it important to understand Jesus' role as both lamb and king?
- What is the second coming of Christ? Why is this event so important within God's plan for human history?
- What do you remember about the three reasons listed in this session for why the world is messed up? How do you respond to that list?
- In what ways will those problems be resolved during the millennium?
- What steps can you take to make your corner of the world—your family and community—more like what you will experience during the millennium?

Use this time to go back and complete any of the study and reflection questions from previous days that you weren't able to finish. Make a note below of any revelations you've had and reflect on any growth or personal insights you've gained.

Read chapters 14–16 in *What Happens Next* before the next group gathering. Use the space below to make note of anything that stands out to you or encourages you.

WEEK 6

BEFORE GROUP MEETING	Read chapters 14–16 in *What Happens Next* Read the Welcome section (page 105)
GROUP MEETING	Discuss the Connect questions Watch the video teaching for session 6 Discuss the questions that follow as a group Do the closing exercise and pray (pages 105–110)
STUDY 1	Complete the personal study (pages 112–114)
STUDY 2	Complete the personal study (pages 115–117)
STUDY 3	Complete the personal study (pages 118–120)
WRAP IT UP	Connect with someone in your group (page 121) Complete any unfinished personal studies Connect with your group about the next study that you want to go through together

THE GREAT HOMECOMING

I saw the Holy City, the new Jerusalem, coming down out of heaven from God, prepared as a bride beautifully dressed for her husband. And I heard a loud voice from the throne saying, "Look! God's dwelling place is now among the people, and he will dwell with them. They will be his people, and God himself will be with them and be their God."

REVELATION 21:2-3

HEAVEN'S
TIME LINE

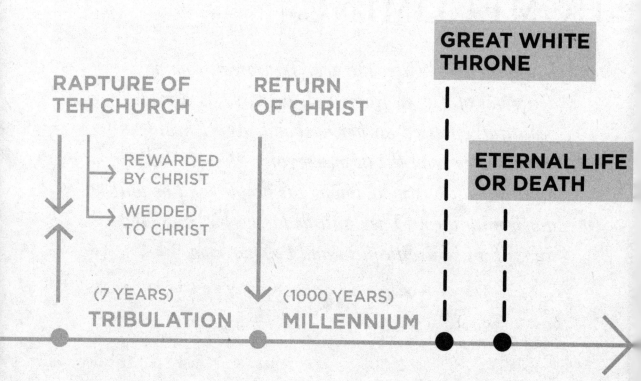

RAPTURE OF TEH CHURCH

REWARDED BY CHRIST

WEDDED TO CHRIST

RETURN OF CHRIST

GREAT WHITE THRONE

ETERNAL LIFE OR DEATH

(7 YEARS)
TRIBULATION

(1000 YEARS)
MILLENNIUM

NOT TO SCALE

WELCOME | READ ON YOUR OWN

Home. It's a simple word. But it carries a weight that cannot be denied. We associate an image and a place when we think of home. It brings up memories, emotions, longings, connections, and other feelings within us. Home is the place where we can finally be ourselves. It's the place where we cast off our fancy clothes, throw on sweatpants, and grab a nap. It's a place of safety, of welcome, of intimacy, and of joy.

Or at least, that is what the term should evoke within us. There are millions of people in our world today who have a far different reaction when they think of the concept of home. For them, home is not a place of safety and security but one of fear, doubt, stress, and danger. Home is a cage from which they long to one day escape.

Isn't it strange that there can be two such different reactions to the same word? Well, the sad reality is that the same will be true about the eternal home we experience at the end of history. For followers of Jesus, our eternal home will be indescribably wonderful—more amazing than anything we have been able to hope or imagine this side of the grave. Eternity in heaven is an eternal blessing.

Yet there is another type of eternal home . . . one called *hell.* Jesus described it as a place of "eternal punishment" (Matthew 25:46). Hell is not something we like to talk about. But it's something that we *must* talk about, because hell is a real place where people will experience a real eternal nightmare of being separated from God. As we will discuss in this final session, hell is as real as heaven—and just as permanent.

CONNECT | 15 MINUTES

Get this session started by choosing one or both of the following questions to discuss together as a group:

- What is something that spoke to you in last week's personal study that you would like to share with the group?

— *or* —

- How would you explain the concept of heaven and hell to a person who had never heard of them before?

WATCH | 20 MINUTES

Now watch the video for this session. Below is an outline of the key points covered during the teaching. Record any key concepts that stand out to you.

OUTLINE

I. When our journey on earth is over, we will find we have never truly been *home* here.
   A. We are "foreigners and exiles" (1 Peter 2:11) who "do not belong to the world" (John 15:19).
   B. Our eternal home is like "a bride beautifully dressed for her husband" (Revelation 21:2 NLT).
   C. In this home, we will never again be separated from our loving heavenly Father.

II. We finally get to say goodbye to Satan forever when we reach our eternal home.
   A. John wrote that after one thousand years, Satan will be released and will once again lead a rebellion on earth, resulting in armies standing in opposition to God.
   B. The battle will end before it begins, and then heaven and earth will be remade anew.
   C. Satan and death itself will finally and forever be cast into the lake of fire.

III. In many ways, the Great White Throne judgment represents the end of human history.
   A. Judgment day begins with the "uncreation" of the world (see Revelation 20:7–10).
   B. Next comes a courtroom scene in which all who rejected Christ are judged according to their works. This is their date with deity.
   C. Those who rejected Christ will spend eternity in hell as a result of their own choice.
   D. Those who accepted Christ will also be judged, but with the caveat that "there is now no condemnation for those who are in Christ Jesus" (Romans 8:1).

IV. The universe will be undone prior to the Great White Throne judgment, so those who have embraced Christ will spend eternity in a recreated world.
   A. God will restore every atom, insect, animal, and galaxy to its original glory.
   B. We will be restarting in the "New Jerusalem" without the consequences of sin.
   C. There will be ample space in the New Jerusalem—plenty of room for billions of people.

V. There will also be plenty of grace in the New Jerusalem.
   A. John stated that the names of Israel's twelve tribes are on New Jerusalem's gates (see Revelation 21:12). Those names include murderers and failures.
   B. John also stated that the names of Jesus' twelve apostles are on the city's foundations (see Revelation 21:14). Those men made countless mistakes and abandoned their Savior.
   C. Ultimately, it is the presence of Jesus that will make New Jerusalem glorious.

NOTES

DISCUSS | 35 MINUTES

Discuss what you just watched by answering the following questions.

1. Paul wrote that "our citizenship is in heaven" (Philippians 3:20). A key element of Christian doctrine is that we are not living in our true home. What are some ways you have felt that discomfort or disconnect from our current world?

2. Ask someone to read aloud Revelation 20:7-10. Not even a thousand years of peace and prosperity in the millennium will cleanse the human heart of its selfish nature. Just as Adam and Eve sinned in a perfect paradise, so a throng of millennium dwellers will do the same. What is your initial reaction when you consider this truth? What are some possible reasons as to why this group of millennium dwellers will choose to side with Satan over Christ?

3. God has declared that "whoever believes in [Jesus] shall not perish but have eternal life" (John 3:16). However, at the Great White Throne judgment, there will be those whose names are "not found written in the book of life" (Revelation 20:15). What can we say about the choices these individuals made to end up there? How is God just basically honoring their preferences?

4. John notes that "on the gates [of the New Jerusalem] were written the names of the twelve tribes of Israel" and that on the city's foundations "were the names of the twelve apostles of the Lamb" (Revelation 21:12, 14). The sons of Jacob were scheming hustlers and liars, while the apostles were often selfish—and they abandoned Jesus on the night of his arrest. Why does God choose to put these names on his holy city? What message does this send about God's grace?

5. Ask someone to read aloud Revelation 21:22-27. What reasons does John provide as to why the New Jerusalem will have no need of a temple or even the sun or moon to give it light? What do you picture when you envision dwelling in such a place filled with God's presence?

RESPOND | 10 MINUTES

The Bible begins with a powerful account of creation, which is vast and cosmic, but then quickly pivots in Genesis 2 to a more intimate description of paradise in the garden of Eden. God is there. Adam and Eve are there. Other creatures, trees, rivers, and even gold are there. It is an idyllic beginning to human history. How fitting, then, that the final chapter of the Bible includes the following detailed picture of our final, eternal home in heaven:

> [1] Then the angel showed me the river of the water of life, as clear as crystal, flowing from the throne of God and of the Lamb [2] down the middle of the great street of the city. On each side of the river stood the tree of life, bearing twelve crops of fruit, yielding its fruit every month. And the leaves of the tree are for the healing of the nations. [3] No longer will there be any curse. The throne of God and of the Lamb will be in the city, and his servants will serve him. [4] They will see his face, and his name will be on their foreheads. [5] There will be no more night. They will not need the light of a lamp or the light of the sun, for the Lord God will give them light. And they will reign for ever and ever.
>
> REVELATION 22:1-5

What are your initial reactions to these verses? What images do you like best—and what emotions do those images evoke?

Where do you see connections and parallels between the garden of Eden and this description of the New Jerusalem? What can we learn about heaven from those connections and parallels?

PRAY | 10 MINUTES

Conclude by thanking God for the privilege of gathering together to study his Word. Thank him for the gift of Scripture, which offers vital information about the future of the world and our lives. Praise God for his goodness in preparing an eternal home for his people. Use the space below to write down any requests so that you and your group members can continue to pray about them in the week ahead.

NAME   **REQUEST**

PERSONAL STUDY

Let's recap *what happens next* when it comes to the end times. At some point in the future, Jesus will rescue his followers in the rapture and take them into Paradise. They will experience the judgment seat of Christ and the marriage supper of the Lamb. But on earth, people will endure the tribulation under the Antichrist. This will end when Jesus returns and establishes the millennium. But this golden age, in turn, will end with another satanic rebellion, the reforming of heaven and earth, and God's eternal judgment on all who reject him. Finally, those who accept Christ as Lord will spend eternity in the heavenly bliss of New Jerusalem. So . . . you have a glorious future ahead of you! As you contemplate this truth during this final personal study, continue to write down your responses to the questions. If you are reading *What Happens Next* alongside this study, first review chapters 14–16 of the book.

A SURPRISING TWIST

As we saw in the previous session, the millennium will be a golden age for humanity. For one thousand years, the people of the earth will experience life without Satan. For one thousand years, all will bask in the presence and the radiance of Jesus. For one thousand years, we will witness righteous rule, prosperity, generosity, and genuine peace between all people.

If you were crafting a novel, you would write "the end" at this point. After all, this sure seems like the *perfect* ending. All of the tension and strife that has driven the story of humanity up to this point appears to now be over in a grand conclusion. It sounds like heaven.

But the millennium will *not* be heaven. Although sin will be greatly diminished on earth because of the absence of Satan and the presence of Christ, it will not be completely removed. We know this because of the plot twist we find near the end of Revelation 20: "When the thousand years are over, Satan will be released from his prison and will go out to deceive the nations in the four corners of the earth—Gog and Magog—and to gather them for battle. In number they are like the sand on the seashore. They marched across the breadth of the earth and surrounded the camp of God's people, the city he loves" (verses 7–9).

Here we go again. Satan, unchained for a short time, will once again do what he has always done: recruit a force of rebels to defy Christ. Who are these people who would dare defy the King? John states they are from "Gog and Magog," which is a term used to describe the enemies of God who live in remote regions (see Ezekiel 38–39). These will be people who are geographically separated from Jesus by distance and generationally separated from the tribulation by time. Far from Jesus. Far from their story. Easy targets for the enemy.

Obviously, this will be a tragic end to the golden age—the thousand years of peace on earth. Rebellion again? War again? Sin again? How could such a thing happen? The answer is *humanity.* Until we are remade, we will still continue to be touched by the corruption of the fall. Even during the millennium, we will still need grace. We will still need a Savior.

1. The earth will witness a thousand years of peace before the release of Satan. What are some reasons why God would allow the devil access to humanity once more?

> [1] Now the serpent was more crafty than any of the wild animals the LORD God had made. He said to the woman, "Did God really say, 'You must not eat from any tree in the garden'?"
>
> [2] The woman said to the serpent, "We may eat fruit from the trees in the garden, [3] but God did say, 'You must not eat fruit from the tree that is in the middle of the garden, and you must not touch it, or you will die.'"
>
> [4] "You will not certainly die," the serpent said to the woman. [5] "For God knows that when you eat from it your eyes will be opened, and you will be like God, knowing good and evil."
>
> [6] When the woman saw that the fruit of the tree was good for food and pleasing to the eye, and also desirable for gaining wisdom, she took some and ate it. She also gave some to her husband, who was with her, and he ate it. [7] Then the eyes of both of them were opened, and they realized they were naked; so they sewed fig leaves together and made coverings for themselves.
>
> GENESIS 3:1–7

2. These verses describe the fall of Adam and Eve. What similarities do you see between the fall and the end of the millennium as described in Revelation 20:7–10?

3. In the words of one scholar, "The source of rebellion against God does not lie in humanity's environment or fundamentally with the devil but springs up from deep within the human heart."[24] How does this explain the fact that people who have experienced peace and prosperity under the reign of Christ will again choose to rebel against him?

4. Read Genesis 3:21–24 to observe some the immediate effects of the fall. When Adam and Eve sinned, they were physically banished from God's presence. This is what sin does—it separates us from a holy God. However, the Bible reveals that God continually reaches out to bring us close once more. Where do you feel God reaching out to you right now?

Our Father has made a vital promise to his children. Before sin was in the heart of humanity, salvation was in the heart of God. God made a covenant. His promises are binding. His decision is fixed. He will have his garden. And we will enjoy it with him. In this world in which everything is upside down, isn't it great to know the world will be right side up?[25]

5. The millennium will reveal not only the depravity in the human heart but also the unending nature of God's sovereignty. He will always accomplish what he has promised to accomplish. Which of God's promises are most important in your life right now? Why?

A SOBER REALITY

Hell. Is there a more startling word in our language? A more depressing idea? A more alarming concept? Just the mention of those four little letters can make us feel deeply uncomfortable. As the theologian C. S. Lewis admitted, "There is no doctrine which I would more willingly remove from Christianity than this, if it lay in my power."[26] We would rather not think of hell.

But the more we try to ignore it, the more the reality stares us in the face. And let's be clear: hell is a reality. We know this based on what Jesus himself said in the Gospels. "Do not be afraid of those who kill the body but cannot kill the soul. Rather, be afraid of the One who can destroy both soul and body in hell" (Matthew 10:28). "If your hand causes you to stumble, cut it off. It is better for you to enter life maimed than with two hands to go into hell, where the fire never goes out" (Mark 9:43). "Whoever believes in the Son has eternal life, but whoever rejects the Son will not see life, for God's wrath remains on them" (John 3:36).

Sobering is too soft a term when describing the reality of hell. Especially when we consider the Bible says "all have sinned" and "the wages of sin is death" (Romans 3:23; 6:23). Every human being, apart from the saving work of Christ, is doomed to spend an eternity cut off from God's presence—an eternity of being completely separated from everything that is good and lovely and beautiful. As Paul wrote, "God is just. . . . He will punish those who do not know God and do not obey the gospel of our Lord Jesus. They will be punished with everlasting destruction and shut out from the presence of the Lord" (2 Thessalonians 1:6, 8–9).

Make no mistake: God doesn't send anyone to hell. Again, in the words of Lewis, "All that are in hell, choose it. Without that self-choice there could be no hell. No soul that seriously and constantly desires joy will ever miss it. Those who seek find."[27] Hell will be populated entirely by volunteers who willingly chose to ignore the repeated warnings of Jesus, the repeated teachings in God's Word, and the repeated witness of the church.

The good news about this bad news is that it need not be our news. Christ has done everything possible to steer us in the direction of heaven. We just need to accept his invitation—and let others in our world know about his invitation as well.

1. Hell is a topic that generates strong opinions and reactions. In what ways have your beliefs about hell changed over time? How would you summarize what you believe about it today?

> [11] Then I saw a great white throne and him who was seated on it. The earth and the heavens fled from his presence, and there was no place for them. [12] And I saw the dead, great and small, standing before the throne, and books were opened. Another book was opened, which is the book of life. The dead were judged according to what they had done as recorded in the books. [13] The sea gave up the dead that were in it, and death and Hades gave up the dead that were in them, and each person was judged according to what they had done. [14] Then death and Hades were thrown into the lake of fire. The lake of fire is the second death. [15] Anyone whose name was not found written in the book of life was thrown into the lake of fire.
>
> REVELATION 20:11–15

2. Underline the words *book* and *books* in the above passage. The *books* that are opened represent the record of people's deeds—the actions of everyone "great and small" who has ever lived.[28] What can you know for certain will happen at the Great White Throne judgment based on these verses? What can you say for certain about God's judgment?

3. Notice in John's account that he calls out one specific *book*—the Book of Life. In ancient times, the names of the citizens in a city were recorded in a register. When the person died, the name was struck out of the book of the living.[29] Given this context, what does it mean for a person's name to not be found written in the Book of Life?

4. Read Revelation 3:5 and Romans 8:31–34. Jesus states that he will never blot out the name of a person in the Book of Life who has found salvation in him. Paul writes that no charge can be brought against those whom God has chosen. What does this reveal about those whose names are found in the Book of Life? What comfort does this give you when you think about all that will transpire at the Great White Throne judgment?

From the first page of Genesis to the final chapter of Revelation . . . God is looking for you. He is searching, waiting, longing for the moment when the two of you will connect and never again separate. He has prepared a new life for you. The word the Bible uses to describe that life is *heaven*.[30]

5. The good news about all this bad news regarding hell is that no one needs to go there. Think of one to three people whom you sense might be on the pathway toward hell—people who, to the best of your knowledge, have rejected the salvation offered by Jesus Christ. What steps will you take to pray for each of those people by name for the next thirty days? What would that require from you?

FINALLY HOME

As we have seen in this final session, hell is a reality that is cemented in the pages of God's Word. It is not something that we can choose to ignore or pretend does not exist. Thankfully, we have equally certain promises in the Bible when it comes to our other option for eternity: *heaven.*

Jesus promised his disciples, "If I go and prepare a place for you, I will come back and take you to be with me that you also may be where I am" (John 14:3). Paul wrote, "We know that if the earthly tent we live in is destroyed, we have a building from God, an eternal house in heaven" (2 Corinthians 5:1). John recorded the following from his vision: "Then I saw 'a new heaven and a new earth,' for the first heaven and the first earth had passed away, and there was no longer any sea. I saw the Holy City, the new Jerusalem, coming down out of heaven from God, prepared as a bride beautifully dressed for her husband" (Revelation 21:1–2).

The dimensions of the Holy City that John goes on to describe are staggering—1,400 miles in length, width, and height. As author Randy Alcorn notes, "We don't need to worry that heaven will be crowded. The ground level of the city will be nearly two million square miles. This is forty times bigger than England and fifteen thousand times bigger than London. It's ten times as big as France or Germany and far larger than India. But remember, that's just the ground level."[31] In the New Jerusalem there will be more than enough room for every believer in Jesus who has ever lived or will ever live. More than enough room for you.

The New Jerusalem will also be perfect. There will be no more pain or suffering. No more death or loss. No more violence or strife. No more sin and no more consequences of sin. "Nothing impure will ever enter it, nor will anyone who does what is shameful or deceitful, but only those whose names are written in the Lamb's book of life" (verse 27).

If you have been saved by the death and resurrection of Jesus Christ, you have a never-ending ticket to this never-ending paradise. So rejoice! Praise your heavenly Father, who is even now preparing that place for you. Live today in anticipation of that glorious tomorrow.

1. Read through John's vision of the New Jerusalem in Revelation 21:9–27. Which of the images catches your attention? What does that image communicate to you?

> [19] "Do not store up for yourselves treasures on earth, where moths and vermin destroy, and where thieves break in and steal. [20] But store up for yourselves treasures in heaven, where moths and vermin do not destroy, and where thieves do not break in and steal. [21] For where your treasure is, there your heart will be also."
>
> MATTHEW 6:19–21

2. Most of us have been taught over and over to live today in a way that reflects the reality of heaven tomorrow—but what does that actually look like? On a practical level, what steps can you take to "store up for [yourself] treasures in heaven"?

3. Heaven is something that followers of Christ often don't think much about. But one truth you should ponder is that heaven is *eternal.* It never ends. This means the decades of your life here on earth are almost inconsequential—they are the very first letter in the story of your life. How could remembering this fact help you now when life gets difficult?

4. Read 1 Peter 2:11–12. Another important truth to ponder about heaven is that it is your real home. What does it mean to live on this earth "as foreigners and exiles"? Why is it vital for you to remember that while you live *in* this world, you are not *of* this world?

Christ has changed your permanent residence. "Think only about the things in heaven" (Colossians 3:2 NCV). . . . "Think about the things of heaven, not the things of earth" (NLT). "Pursue the things over which Christ presides" (MSG). These translations combine to declare in one verse: live in the light of heaven!

How heaven-minded are you? . . . A day with no thought of heaven is a day poorly used. The soul needs hourly gazes into the life to come. You need to know what your departed loved ones are doing. We need to envision the rapture and the millennium. Let's imagine the New Jerusalem and the face of God. Heaven is the green vegetable in the spiritual diet. Be consumed with the things above.[32]

5. God has revealed the promises of heaven to you for a reason. So, as you conclude this study, consider how you would answer that question: *How heaven-minded are you?* What steps would you need to take in your day to become a more heaven-minded person?

WRAP IT UP

Connect with a group member and talk about some of the insights from this final session. Use any of the prompts below to guide your discussion.

- The millennium will be a golden age of peace, but it will end in an experience similar to the fall recorded in Genesis 3. What does that reality teach you about the relationship between humanity and God?
- How did this session add to your understanding about hell?
- How did this session add to your understanding of the New Jerusalem?
- What are some of the topics you would like to explore in more detail (or questions you would like to have answered) as you conclude this study?
- Who is someone in your life who would benefit from the content in this study? What steps can you take to explore it with that person?

Use this time to go back and complete any of the study and reflection questions from previous days that you weren't able to finish. Make note of what God has revealed to you in these days. Finally, talk with your group about what study you may want to go through next. Put a date on the calendar for when you'll meet next to study God's Word and dive deeper into community.

LEADER'S GUIDE

Thank you for your willingness to lead your group through this study! What you have chosen to do is valuable and will make a difference in the lives of others. *What Happens Next* is a six-session Bible study built around video content and small-group interaction. As the group leader, imagine yourself as the host of a party. Your job is to take care of your guests by managing the details so that when your guests arrive, they can focus on one another and on the interaction around the topic for that session.

Your role as the group leader is not to answer all the questions or reteach the content—the video, book, and study guide will do most of that work. Your job is to guide the experience and cultivate your small group into a connected and engaged community. This will make it a place for members to process, question, and reflect—not necessarily to receive more instruction. There are several elements in this leader's guide that will help you as you structure your study and reflection time, so be sure to follow along and take advantage of each one.

BEFORE YOU BEGIN

Before your first meeting, make sure the group members have a copy of this study guide. Alternately, you can hand out the study guides at your first meeting and give the members some time to look over the material and ask any preliminary questions. Also, make sure that the group members are aware that they have access to the streaming videos at any time by following the instructions provided with this guide. During your first meeting, ask the members to provide their names, phone numbers, and email addresses so that you can keep in touch with them.

Generally, the ideal size for a group is eight to ten people, which will ensure that everyone has enough time to participate in discussions. If you have more people, break up the main group into smaller subgroups. Encourage those who show up at the first meeting to commit to attending the duration of the study, as this will help the group members get to know one another, create stability for the group, and help you know how best to prepare to lead the participants through the material.

Each session begins with an opening reflection in the Welcome section. The questions that follow in the Connect section serve as icebreakers to get the group members thinking about the topic. In the rest of the study, it's generally not a good idea to have everyone answer every question—a free-flowing discussion is more desirable. But with the icebreaker question, you can go around the circle and ask each person to respond. Encourage shy people to share, but don't force them.

At your first meeting, let the group members know that each session also contains a personal study section that they can use to continue to engage with the content until the next meeting. While doing this section is optional, it will help participants cement the concepts presented during the group study time and help them better understand how humility will help them see God, themselves, and others more accurately.

Let them know that if they choose to do so, they can watch the video for the next session by accessing the streaming code provided with this study guide. Invite them to bring any questions and insights to your next meeting, especially if they had a breakthrough moment or didn't understand something.

PREPARATION FOR EACH SESSION

As the leader, there are a few things you should do to best prepare for each meeting:

- **Read through the session.** This will help you become more familiar with the content and know how to structure the discussion times.
- **Decide how the videos will be used.** Determine whether you want the members to watch the videos ahead of time (again, via the streaming access code provided with this study guide) or together as a group.
- **Decide which questions you want to discuss.** Based on the length of your group discussions, you may not be able to get through all the questions. So look over the discussion questions provided in each session and mark which ones you definitely want to cover.
- **Be familiar with the questions you want to discuss.** When the group meets, you'll be watching the clock, so make sure you are familiar with the questions you have selected.
- **Pray for your group.** Pray for your group members and ask God to lead them as they study his Word and listen to his Spirit.

In many cases, there will be no one "right" answer to the questions. Answers will vary, especially when the group members are sharing their personal experiences.

STRUCTURING THE DISCUSSION TIME

You will need to determine with your group how long you want your meetings to last so that you can plan your time accordingly. Suggested times for each section have been provided in this study guide, and if you adhere to these times, your group will meet for ninety minutes. However, many groups like to meet for two hours. If this describes your particular group, follow the times listed in the right-hand column of the chart given below.

Section	90 Minutes	120 Minutes
CONNECT (discuss one or more of the opening questions for the session)	15 minutes	20 minutes
WATCH (watch the teaching material together and take notes)	20 minutes	20 minutes
DISCUSS (discuss the study questions you selected ahead of time)	35 minutes	50 minutes
RESPOND (write down key takeaways)	10 minutes	15 minutes
PRAY (pray together and dismiss)	10 minutes	15 minutes

As the group leader, it is up to you to keep track of the time and to keep things on schedule. You might want to set a timer for each segment so that both you and the group members know when the time is up. (There are some good phone apps for timers that play a gentle chime or other pleasant sound instead of a disruptive noise.)

Don't be concerned if group members are quiet or slow to share. People are often quiet when they are pulling together their ideas, and this might be a new experience for some of them. Just ask a question and let it hang in the air until someone shares. You can then say, "Thank you. What about others? What came to you when you watched that portion of the teaching?"

GROUP DYNAMICS

Leading a group through *What Happens Next* will prove to be highly rewarding both to you and your group members. But you still may encounter challenges along the way! Discussions can get off track. Group members may not be sensitive to the needs and ideas of others. Some might worry that they will be expected to talk about matters that make them feel awkward. Others may express comments that result in disagreements.

To help ease this strain on you and the group, consider the following ground rules:

- When someone raises a question or comment that is off the main topic, suggest you deal with it another time, or, if you feel led to go in that direction, let the group know that you will be spending some time discussing it.
- If someone asks a question that you don't know how to answer, admit it and move on. At your discretion, feel free to invite group members to comment on questions that call for personal experience.
- If you find that one or two people are dominating the discussion time, direct a few questions to others in the group. Outside the main group time, ask the more dominating members to help you draw out the quieter ones. Work to make them part of the solution instead of part of the problem.
- When a disagreement occurs, encourage the group members to process the matter in love. Encourage those on opposite sides to restate what they heard the other side say about the matter, and then invite each side to evaluate if that perception is accurate. Lead the group in examining other passages related to the topic and look for common ground.

When any of these issues arise, encourage your group members to follow these words from Scripture: "Love one another" (John 13:34); "If it is possible, as far as it depends on you, live at peace with everyone" (Romans 12:18); "Whatever is true . . . noble . . . right . . . pure . . . lovely . . . if anything is excellent or praiseworthy—think about such things" (Philippians 4:8); and, "Everyone should be quick to listen, slow to speak and slow to become angry" (James 1:19). This will make your group time more rewarding and beneficial for everyone who attends.

Thank you for taking the time to lead your group. You are making a difference in your group members' lives and having an impact on their journey toward a better understanding of how they can know *what happens next* in God's time line of history.

NOTES

1. David Jeremiah, *The Book of Signs* (Nashville, TN: W Publishing, 2019), 183.
2. Max Lucado, *What Happens Next* (Nashville, TN: Nelson Books, 2024), 5–6.
3. Lucado, *What Happens Next,* 12.
4. Lucado, *What Happens Next*, 20.
5. Lucado, *What Happens Next*, 23.
6. Lucado, *What Happens Next*, 48.
7. Lucado, *What Happens Next*, 53–54.
8. Joseph Henry Thayer, *Thayer's Greek Lexicon* (1841), s.v. *bēma*. See the use of the word in Matthew 27:19; John 19:13; Acts 18:12, 16–17; 25:6, 10, 17; Romans 14:10; and 2 Corinthians 5:10.
9. Lucado, *What Happens Next*, 71.
10. Merriam-Webster's Dictionary, s.v. "purgatory," https://www.merriam-webster.com/dictionary/purgatory#:~:text=purgatory-,noun,of%20their%20sins%20by%20suffering.
11. James Strong, *harpazō*, G726. See also Matthew 13:19 ("snatches away"); John 10:28 ("snatch them"); Acts 8:39 ("took . . . away"); and Revelation 12:5 ("snatched up").
12. Lucado, *What Happens Next*, 86–87.
13. This is a bit of a trick question, in that Jesus also endured a physical death on the cross and "was raised on the third day" (1 Corinthians 15:4). The events in Acts 1:1–11 record his subsequent ascension into heaven.
14. Lucado, *What Happens Next*, 101.
15. Lucado, *What Happens Next*, 110, 112.
16. Lucado, *What Happens Next*, 119.
17. David J. MacLeod, "The Lion Who Is a Lamb: An Exposition of Revelation 5:1–7," Bibliotheca Sacra (July–September 2007): 325–330, cited by Mark Hitchcock, *The End: Everything You'll Want to Know About the Apocalypse* (Carol Stream, IL: Tyndale, 2018), 78; Amir Tsafarti, *Revealing Revelation* (Harvest Prophecy, 2022), 84; Charles Swindoll, *Living Insights New Testament Commentary: Revelation* (Tyndale House, 2014), 102.
18. Lucado, *What Happens Next*, 131–133.
19. John Blanchard, *Whatever Happened to Hell?* (Wheaton, IL: Crossway Books), 93.
20. Lucado, *What Happens Next*, 143.
21. "Modeling the Future of Religion in America," Pew Research Center, September 13, 2022, https://www.pewresearch.org/religion/2022/09/13/modeling-the-future-of-religion-in-america/; John Blake, "Predictions About the Decline of Christianity in America May Be Premature," CNN, April 9, 2023, https://www.cnn.com/2023/04/08/us/christianity-decline-easter-blake-cec/index.html.
22. Lucado, *What Happens Next*, 146–147.
23. Lucado, *What Happens Next*, 150.
24. Alan F. Johnson, *The Expositor's Bible Commentary: Revelation* (Grand Rapids, MI: Zondervan Academic, 2006), 772.
25. Lucado, *What Happens Next*, 154–155.
26. C. S. Lewis, *The Problem of Pain* (London: Geoffrey Bles, 1940), 94.

27. Lewis, *The Great Divorce* (London: Geoffrey Bles, 1945).

28. Johnson, *The Expositor's Bible Commentary: Revelation*, 775.

29. Johnson, *The Expositor's Bible Commentary: Revelation*, 629.

30. Lucado, *What Happens Next*, 168.

31. Randy Alcorn, "What Are the New Jerusalem's Dimensions?" Eternal Perspective Ministries, February 22, 2010, https://www.epm.org/resources/2010/Feb/22/what-are-new-jerusalems-dimensions/.

32. Lucado, *What Happens Next*, 184.

ABOUT THE AUTHOR

Since entering the ministry in 1978, Max Lucado has served churches in Miami, Florida; Rio de Janeiro, Brazil; and San Antonio, Texas. He currently serves as the teaching minister of Oak Hills Church in San Antonio. He is the recipient of the 2021 ECPA Pinnacle Award for his outstanding contribution to the publishing industry and society at large. He is America's bestselling inspirational author with more than 150 million products in print. Visit his website at MaxLucado.co

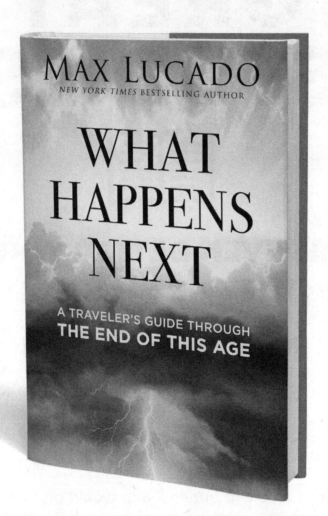